THE UNE[illegible] STRUGGLE

THE FINDINGS OF A WESTINDIAN RESEARCH INVESTIGATION INTO THE UNDERACHIEVEMENT OF WESTINDIAN CHILDREN IN BRITISH SCHOOLS

by Ashton Gibson

assistant author: Jocelyn Barrow

Published by Centre for Caribbean Studies, Caribbean House, Bridport Place, London N1 5DS

First published 1986

British Library Cataloguing in Publication Data

Gibson, Ashton
The unequal struggle: an educational research into the underachievement of West Indian children.
1. West Indians -Education - Great Britain
2. Academic achievement
I. Title II. Centre for Caribbean Studies
371.97′969729′041 LC2806.G7

ISBN 0 948477 02 4 (cloth)
ISBN 0 948477 03 2 (paper)

Typeset by Photosetting, 6 Foundry House, Stars Lane, Yeovil, Somerset BA20 1NL. Telephone Yeovil 23684

Printed in Great Britain by Unwin Brothers, Gresham Press, Old Woking, Surrey GU22 9LH

Object of the research

The investigation set out to answer three questions:

1. Why are Westindian teenagers underachieving at school and at work?
2. What lies behind their indifference to society and their parents?
3. What determines their attitudes, responses and lifestyles?

Method of inquiry

Informal oral interviews on tape; information substantiated by evidence from a variety of other profiles and sources.

Interviewee statistics

Westindians aged 13 – 16, at school	308
Westindians aged 16 – 19, at school	41
Westindians aged 16 – 19, employed	68
Westindians aged 16 – 19, unemployed	91
Total number of Westindian teenagers interviewed	508

Contents

PART 4 - POSTSCRIPT

Acknowledgements

I wish to express my sincere appreciation to the following for the help they so generously gave in getting the project off the ground, almost all of them by contributing directly to the training of our interviewers. The details in brackets concern their position or sphere of work at the time of their involvement with the training programme.

Hal Austin (former Editor, *Roots* Magazine)
David Bamber (Chief Research Officer, LB Hackney)
The Hon Mark Bonham Carter (former Deputy Director-General, BBC)
John Blyth (Development & Planning Director, LB Hackney)
Clinton Davis (former MP for Hackney Central)
Fred Francis (former Manager, Hackney Jobcentre)
The Rt Rev Victor Guazelli (Catholic Bishop of Westminster in East London)
Rev John Hastings (Methodist Church, Division of Social Responsibility)
Ronald Howell (Magistrate/Chairman, Juvenile Court)
Joy Leitch (Teacher Training, Language)
The Earl of Longford (Publisher)
Anna MacDonald (Manpower Services Commission, Special Programmes Division)
Alan McFarlane (Senior Housing Adviser, LB Hackney)
Spencer Millham (Director, Dartington Social Research Unit)
Commander David Mitchell (Metropolitan Police)
Chief Supt Mulligan (Metropolitan Police)
Prof Roy Parker (School of Applied Social Studies, Bristol University)
Michael Round, (School Headmaster, LB Croydon)
Andrew Rowe M.P.
Olsen Samuels (former Social Services, LB Hackney)
Daphne Stewart (Senior Careers Officer, ILEA)
Mary Sugden (former Director, Social Services, LB Hackney)
Susan Weil (former National Foster Care Association officer)

I am most grateful to *Caribbean Times* and Caribbean Chamber of Commerce for providing short-term placement facilities which enabled us to observe trainee interviewers under normal working conditions.

Eglon Whittingham did much to broaden my understanding and insight with regard to attitudes and their significance. I should also like to acknowledge the part played by Charles Lewis, writer-in-residence at the Centre for Caribbean Studies and my co-author on Caribbean House's 10th anniversary volume, *A Light in the Dark Tunnel*, in editing and preparing these findings for publication.

Finally, I received unstinting support from Sir Hugh Springer, KCMG (now Governor-General of Barbados) and Keith Barker, former director and current director respectively of Caribbean House; and above all from my assistant author, Jocelyn Barrow, who helped to define our methodology and did so much of the sifting, analysing and evaluating of the mountain of material.

A.G.

Foreword

Profile of the Author

Ashton Gibson is a soft-spoken, articulate man who came to Britain from Barbados as a 25-year-old in the early 1950s. His serious face and furrowed brow reflect the profound compassion and concern he feels for his fellow Westindians in their continuing struggle to adjust to life in the 'Promised Land'. Occasionally the lined features break into an impish grin, even a loud chuckle; despite the oceans of tragedy and injustice he has seen, both in his personal life and in the lives of those he tries to help, his sense of humour has not deserted him. It would take more than an ocean to douse the genial Caribbean spirit in him altogether.

What marks Ashton Gibson out as a remarkable person is not the fact that he has devoted his life to serving others, nor that he has moved mountains in the attempt to secure a better deal for his fellows, to say nothing of his many noteworthy achievements and experiences (for the full story the reader is referred to the introduction to Caribbean House's 10th anniversary volume, *A Light in the Dark Tunnel*). His extra-special quality is his unwavering firmness of purpose despite all the difficulties that beleaguer him. This intrinsic strength is typified by his steadfast refusal to stoop to pettiness in the face of deep-rooted prejudice and severe ill-will, and is founded on an indestructible faith in the healing power of love and tolerance.

A man in his position inevitably has enemies both outside and within his own community, since fear – conspicuous by its absence in Dr. Gibson – is the all-too-common arbiter of response to the issues which he is willing to tackle head-on. He has been vilified and condemned from all sides, irrespective of race, colour or creed. Whether it be the White-dominated Establishment, or Black activists, or Race Relations specialists, many find Ashton Gibson and his enlightened approach hard to live with. Quite undaunted, he continues to speak his mind and to take whatever action humanity and common sense dictate.

The aims of the organisations which he has founded, and which reflect his chosen path, are centred around one all-important principle: the overwhelming need for Westindians to provide counselling, care and succour to others from the Westindian community in greater need than themselves. There are any number of ways to approach this, and thus each of the various organisations based at Caribbean House has a different emphasis. Ashton Gibson believes in strongly maintaining all-round support for those who have proved unable to cope. Perhaps his most controversial scheme has been the so-called 'Homeward Bound' Fund, which was launched with a view to helping those desperate souls for whom return to the Caribbean represented a glimmer of hope in otherwise barren and unchangeable circumstances. It was an entirely humanitarian gesture aimed at a tiny percentage of the Westindian community in Britain, but once others – less charitably-minded – got hold of the idea, it became an enormity. His least malicious critics called him politically naive to imagine that such a scheme was not playing into the hands of racist agitators. The hard-liners called into question his very credibility as a spokesman for Westindians in Britain.

What does give Ashton Gibson the right to speak on behalf of his community? The answer to that lies in his background and in his character; not, assuredly, in any pieces of paper or tokens of Establishment approval. Experience has taught him that the stress of being a 'fish out of water' – a common feeling among Britain's Westindians, though largely unacknowledged even by themselves – can lead to erratic, anti-social and eventually violent behaviour, which in turn leads to incarceration either in a mental hospital or in jail. After years of repeated problems of this kind, Ashton Gibson transformed his life by turning his self-destructive energy into positive and life-enhancing efforts on behalf of those whose problems he most understood. He founded 'Melting Pot' in Brixton, and after his successful pioneering work there moved on in 1975 to the London Borough of Hackney, where the organisations collectively known as Caribbean House are still flourishing under his inspired direction.

But his dreams will not have been fulfilled until these community enterprises, astonishingly effective as they have proved in helping Westindian families in Hackney (and beyond in some cases) can transcend the barriers of racial hatred, distrust and discrimination, and reach out to a wider public. This involves more than just reinforcing the ethnic identity of Britain's Westindians; the rest of the public, professionals in particular, must be helped to understand the meaning of that identity within the context of a multi-racial and multi-cultural society. Such aims require no plaudits or recognition in themselves. All they call for is responsive and responsible action on the part of all concerned, in order to create a better climate for everyone to live in.

Come face to face with him and you cannot fail to be deeply impressed by Ashton Gibson's insight, compassion and integrity, to which this book bears eloquent testimony. It is perhaps for this reason that his enemies keep their distance.

Charles Lewis
(co-author, with Ashton Gibson,
of *A Light in the Dark Tunnel*)

Rev. Dr. Ashton Gibson, LHD, D Soc Psychol, is Director-General of Caribbean House (see Appendix A).

Assistant author Jocelyn Barrow, OBE, MA, is an educationalist who has worked extensively in schools and teacher education. She is also a member of the Community Relations Council, a Governor of the BBC, and Chairman of Caribbean House Group.

Introduction

I am a Westindian. I know something of Westindian life on its home ground – its values, its culture, its style. When I set out to discover the factors lying behind the underachievement of Westindian children in British schools, I must confess that I was not prepared for what I eventually found. It distresses me to write up this research.

In addition to the two years of intensive work collecting and analysing data, it took another three years for me to muster enough courage to publish the research findings. I have endeavoured to present them with honesty and accuracy, and it is my earnest hope that they will cause the least possible distress to the Westindian community. There is nothing in these pages that cannot be substantiated factually. But I cannot say that I expect to be believed.

The research itself was a major undertaking involving detailed and informed investigation of a matter directly affecting the future welfare of the Westindian community in Britain. It is by no means the first such survey to be undertaken in this country, but it has a number of unique characteristics that set it apart from anything hitherto attempted. The most important of these is the fact that it was conducted by myself – a Westindian – and that I was assisted by another Westindian, Miss Jocelyn Barrow, and the field work was carried out by eight Westindian research assistants who had to put in 12 hours a day for over two years gathering a wealth of data. It was indeed an achievement that we were able to obtain the full cooperation of the numerous Westindian teenagers and their families who took part in this comprehensive research programme.

It is our hope that the results presented here will be thought-provoking and conducive to a better understanding of the nature and size of the problems facing Westindian children. What comes across to the reader, we trust, is neither anger nor antagonism, but rather a sense of urgency that something must be done.

A.G.

Social science surveys are normally carried out on the basis of large-scale questionnaire studies and analysis of the data collected in them. Such traditional methodology could not, however, be used for our own research. The special nature of the subject demanded a rather different approach, involving collation of information from a variety of sources in order to arrive at a consistent story in each case.

For this reason we decided to gather our information from three different profiles: the individual, the family, and the school or place of employment. Each interview was tape-recorded and consisted of three separate two-hour sessions with the teenage subject in each of these contexts. Our research assistants had to undergo an intensive three-month training course to develop interviewing skills and to enable them to obtain the maximum response from interviewees. We had to overcome the fact that Westindians find it very difficult to volunteer information about themselves if they think it will show them up in a bad light. The true picture often emerged only after the three separate profiles had been linked together.

Some of the information was gathered through the use of a technique successfully employed by British Intelligence during World War II. It was very difficult to extract any information from German airmen captured after being shot down over Britain; they were often ultra-defensive and gave only their name, rank and serial number as required of them by the Geneva Convention. The device developed by Intelligence was to approach these men in a social welfare register, offering – for example – to notify their families that they were safe. This yielded a wealth of information that proved useful to the Allies.

After listening to every interview and studying all that emerged from them – beyond the words and the silences, the mucking about and the sheer bravado – we knew that there was one factor above all others that could no longer be disguised. Most of the teenagers were finding it very difficult indeed to cope with being Black in Britain, and many were in fact suffering from severe stress. To satisfy ourselves that we had indeed reached the correct conclusion, we had to listen to and study all the recordings again – a substantial undertaking.

We were up against the fact that the methodology had not been designed to reveal the stress factor. For, even in the light of the appalling disadvantage and discomfort experienced by their parents, it had not been envisaged that Westindian schoolchildren in Britain could be under such a degree of stress as a group. How could children who had barely begun life, who as yet had no responsibility, be associated with a mental condition that conjured up so much superstition and fear among Westindians? We have endeavoured to provide an answer to this and, indeed, to many other pertinent questions within these pages.

These research findings will no doubt be challenged and the methodology decried by those who have nothing better to do than snipe at the efforts of others without bothering to see what lessons can be learned. The conclusions stand or fall, in our view, by their relevance to the situation as it exists. So to our critics we say: pull the findings apart by all means – but ignore them at your peril. We need hardly add that recent events in Handsworth, Brixton and Tottenham have spelt out – for ostriches and extremists alike – just what that peril is.

A.G.
J.B.

PART 1

THE WESTINDIAN PERSPECTIVE

The Culture of the Westindian Child

Anyone setting out to identify the causes of underachievement among Westindians in British schools must first have some knowledge of Westindian children and their culture. This is crucial if the matter under investigation is to be seen in its true perspective.

Firstly, although a considerable number of Westindians are of European, Indian or Chinese descent,* we are primarily concerned here with the descendants of the African slaves brought to the Caribbean in former times. These represent a substantial majority among the peoples of the Caribbean, and are generally referred to as the Afro-Caribbean or Black community. Secondly, by 'Westindian children' we mean those of Westindian stock, irrespective of whether they or their parents were born outside the Caribbean.

A sense of cultural identity is generally lacking in people from the Caribbean, a legacy of over 200 years of slavery endured by their forefathers. Although the highly oppressive conditions imposed on the slaves inevitably dictated the way they lived, it was their slave-master's way of life that they regarded as the ideal model. Over the years their situation remained essentially the same, and what had originally been a temporary and improvised *modus vivendi* gradually became an acquired lifestyle of a more permanent nature. The slaves never valued a structure of living which they had embraced solely for the purposes of surviving the cruel rigours of slavery. But it became deeply rooted, nevertheless, for want of an available alternative over a long period.

The net result was that when emancipation finally came, bringing with it conditions that were little advance on slavery,

---

* Asian labourers were first brought to the Caribbean under the indenture system, introduced when slavery was abolished there in 1834. Many of them became permanent settlers.

there was scant alteration to the established pattern. Since then, successive generations have carried on most of the traditions and attitudes handed down to them by their parents, while continuing to be ashamed of the life their ancestors lived and therefore attaching no cultural significance to it.

Most Westindians would therefore deny that they have a culture at all; only a small minority have rediscovered their African roots (for example, the Rastafarian movement). Having failed to emulate the lifestyle which was the privilege of the slave-master's children, they see themselves as cultureless. This amounts to an identity crisis which has undermined the confidence of Westindian adults, and they in turn have found themselves unable to inspire confidence and a sense of identity in the young, who badly need it to help them in their development – especially in Britain.

Whether or not it is recognised by those who are a part of it, the fact remains that there is a culture with a distinct flavour of its own in the Caribbean. What is more, it works and has many positive values which make it in some ways superior to the sophisticated European culture after which they hanker. It is a caring and sharing culture in which sensitivity towards the individual is paramount and all responsibility – even that of parenthood – is shared not only with other members of the family but with friends as well.

Within the mainstream of European sociology there has been a complete denial of the specific experience of the Westindian, the experience of a people uprooted from their native Africa and taken in bondage to the Caribbean. The fact that this mass transplantation was brought about by Europeans, an atrocity for which their descendants have conveniently abdicated their historical accountability, is a side issue which need not concern us here. What is important to realise, however, is that whilst the theories of Freud, Durkheim and others go a long way towards explaining certain phenomena, such commentators represent a strictly European cultural viewpoint. Their paradigms and conclusions are therefore necessarily rooted within that framework.

Precisely how long after emancipation the offspring of slave stock began to be called Westindians is a matter of purely academic interest. The incontrovertible fact is that out of their extraordinary experience of living under the cheerless and inhuman conditions of slavery there developed a culture, a language, a psychology and a symbolism known only to them – and which only a Westindian can perceive, comprehend and respond to (though many are reluctant to do so for reasons described above). The study of these characteristics, and of that distinct area of historical, political and social development which is relevant to Westindians, may be termed Westindian sociology.

It is our contention that anyone looking for solutions to problems among Westindians, born in the Caribbean or elsewhere, must have a firm grasp of Westindian sociology. It is a sociological fact that every human being is totally dependent on others at birth, and that every society provides some form of family unit to take care of the infant. This has always meant that the family, and not the geographical location (though that, too, is important), is the most pervasive influence in determining a child's cultural identity.

In considering the performance of Westindian children in British schools, this is possibly the most crucial factor to be taken into account. Yet it continues to be minimised, if not dismissed altogether, by those whose opinions count where the Establishment is concerned.

The Westindian Family

A significant aspect of slavery, in some ways its most important legacy, is that unity of any kind was strenuously discouraged. Family life was therefore forbidden to the slaves while remaining the prerogative of the slave-owner. Like many other features of the latter's life, the European family model became the ideal to which all aspired after emancipation. As a result, the Westindian family structure of today is full of contradictions.

In Britain the two-parent nuclear family is standard and any other form of family is regarded either as a misfortune or as an affront to dignity – this in spite of the so-called 'permissive society', which is as conservative as anything that preceded it. In the Caribbean, however, and among Westindians in Britain, there are three main models: the unmarried mother, the common-law marriage, and the formal marriage.

The Unmarried Mother

The unmarried mother is an accepted institution among Westindians, and accounts for some 65% of all families of Afro-Caribbean origins, with the exception of St. Lucia, Grenada and Dominica, because of strong Catholic influences. The term 'single parent family', as it is known in the UK, is not used in the Caribbean because unmarried mothers can invariably rely on their own mothers, as well as aunts and other relatives, to help them bring up their children. This informal system, a long-standing tradition, is known as the 'extended family'. No stigma is attached to any member of the family grouping, and no social distinction is made between children of the same mother by different fathers. However, in 1966 Barbados passed a law enabling illegitimate children to inherit from their father or to contest their father's will. Jamaica followed suit in 1974.

Common-Law Marriage

In theory most Westindians regard formal marriage as the only proper and legal foundation for family life. In practice, however, there is a tendency to enter into a cohabiting arrangement, familiarly known as 'living with' someone and officially termed 'common-law marriage'. Such marriages entail the same rights as a formal marriage, but while the man will support the family as best he can, the wife/mother will definitely be expected to help by going out to work. The relationship is usually seen and treated as a temporary arrangement by both partners. It may last for years and eventually develop into a formal marriage, or the couple may break up after a comparatively short time together.

Formal Marriage

Notwithstanding the prevalence of the above institutions, formal marriage – the model provided by the slave-owners of former days – is still considered the ideal for family life among Westindians. The father is regarded as the head of the household and the chief provider. His wife may help by going out to work, but she is not obliged or expected to do so.

For all its legality and superficial respectability, formal marriage rarely brings out the most positive virtues of Westindian family culture in those who embrace it. The brazen or thinly-disguised licentiousness of the slave-owners, almost all of them married men, has similarly left its mark on succeeding generations of Westindian males. Thus, while prizing formal marriage far above all other relationships, many of them have little or no respect for the constraints it is supposed to place on them, legal or spiritual. Couples may genuinely try to follow the self-centred European nuclear family model, but sharing and general involvement with other members of the extended family is so culturally rooted that a wife can seldom monopolise her husband's services, and she may well find it hard to compete with her mother-in-law for his affection.

Child-Rearing

One of the culture clashes that affects Westindians in Britain particularly adversely is the difference between their child-rearing practices and those of the indigenous population. The upbringing of Westindian children is a paradoxical mixture of extreme permissiveness and extreme strictness. Scolding and punishment are often meted out in inconsistent and apparently arbitrary fashion, and this tends to hamper the development of sound principles and good habits. And because they are rarely given reasons for the things they are told to do (another legacy of slavery), they are often lacking in reasoning ability.

The Caribbean has very little tradition of toys or other man-made play materials, which are quite unnecessary where there is an abundance of natural resources, such as sea, sand, rocks and trees, as well as animals and birds. These things not only stimulate the imagination but also aid the development of certain basic skills – skills in which Westindians brought up in Britain are generally deficient.

Most Westindian parents expect their children to help with housework, yet another attitude traceable to the days of slavery when children as young as five or six years of age were required to work in the fields, and childhood was not valued for its own sake but treated as an apprenticeship culminating in graduation to full membership of the slave-master's labour force. The demands increase as the youngsters grow older, and girls are called upon to look after their younger brothers and sisters. Children of either sex, therefore, have little opportunity to develop as individuals who are not dependent on the group. But they are, nevertheless, expected to cope with multiple conflicting pressures, to operate in a register which is quite alien to them, to be obedient and hardworking in the home and also to excel academically outside it, to succeed in the big, tough world without being given the tools to do so. And when they attempt to break out on their own, they are accused of being bad and ungrateful.

Such a situation could well lead to a child being taken into care in Britain, and perhaps rightly so if he or she were a member of the indigenous population. But in the Westindian family context this would be regarded as quite normal and tolerable, with the vast majority of cases being resolved in due course. Teachers and social workers often conspire – with the very best of intentions – to take Westindian children away from their families, in the erroneous belief that they are helping the child's development. Unfortunately, the very reverse occurs and few sociologists would deny that the arbitrary removal of Westindian children from their homes has played a significant part in the social unrest which manifested itself in the riots of Toxteth and Brixton in 1981, and of Handsworth, Brixton and Tottenham in 1985. These were mercifully brief eruptions, but if the present trend is allowed to continue there can be little doubt that it will pose even greater social problems in the future.

Migration and After

A tragedy second only to slavery in its terrible consequences for the Westindian people was the post-war wave of migration to the United Kingdom. The vast majority who made that fateful trek across the Atlantic had not the remotest idea of what life in Britain would be like, and certainly did not know how to go about fitting in once they had arrived. All they knew was that they were sailing to the 'Motherland'. Some may have blithely assumed they would be welcomed, but in general no-one gave a thought to the kind of reception they would get or to the attitude of the British people.

Their main reason for coming was the prospect of employment, since jobs were very scarce in the Caribbean (and therefore few had ever done any formal work). The sugar economy, developed with the commandeered aid of their forefathers, could no longer sustain them and had virtually collapsed in many of the islands. Post-war Britain was in need of extra labour, and people from the Commonwealth were being urged – by Enoch Powell, among others – to come and fill the many vacancies, especially in transport and the health service. Many of the newcomers settled in London or Birmingham, where there were most jobs to be had. Unlike other immigrant groups, they did not form close-knit communities and took a very long time to establish even a semblance of cultural and ethnic identity. A large number saw themselves as migrant labour, and expected to return to the Caribbean after improving their education or acquiring professional or technical qualifications which would increase their work prospects at home. Alternatively their sights were set on amassing enough capital to shake off the lowly economic status that was their lot. Thus commitment to becoming involved in the political or social life of the UK – let alone ability to do so – was lacking in the majority, a lack which continues to prevail even today.

Coping with life in a complex and sophisticated urban environment was always likely to be difficult for the average Westindian accustomed to life on a tropical island – a life involving many attitudes and tendencies traceable to the days of slavery, including the need to be given clear direction. Yet they were left to make their own arrangements for settling in entirely unaided, a piece of gross negligence on the part of the host country which ensured that they not only started at the very bottom of British society but have remained trapped there. Over the years the Westindian community has, if anything, become even more entrenched in this disadvantaged position, this murky backwater where all the benefits of the mainstream inevitably pass them by. A few individuals have managed to carve a niche for themselves, mostly at the expense of their pride or their principles (i.e., they have successfully 'aped' the White man), but the overwhelming majority have been unable to make any headway because they have lacked the necessary tools.

This is where schools come in. It is one thing for Westindians to settle for low-paid, unskilled work while others cream off the best jobs; it is quite another for the education system to perpetuate the *status quo* by consistently failing to meet the needs of Westindian children. Above all, teachers have not been given the training they need to help them understand these children who, while apparently speaking something resembling English, come from a vastly different cultural world with a language and a conceptual system very much its own (this issue is dealt with in more detail on pp. 99–104).

For a long time it has been one of the great myths among British educationalists, politicians and race relations officers that all the early problems were transitional; that nothing needed to be done to help first-generation Westindian migrants, and that difficulties were only to be expected when children were transplanted from the Caribbean to schools in Britain half-way through their education. That myth has now been finally and conclusively exploded. Events have shown that Westindians born in this country have fared, and are still faring, even worse than the migrants did – in education and, indeed, every other sphere of life in Britain.

It is frequently argued, of course, that there have been comparable migrations to the UK from other parts of the world – especially Asia – and that the effects should therefore be essentially the same. In answer to this, one need only quote from the Swann Report (dealt with in the next section), which sums up this particular issue and its implications for the British educational system with admirable succinctness:

'. . . it should be recalled that the nature of the West Indian and the Asian migrations were significantly different, the one arising from the largely rural, colonial hierarchy of island economies, the other deriving from the more diversified labour market of a colonial administration run more on partnership with the established social system. It would therefore be no surprise if attitudes to education and the acquisition of qualifications were to vary between West Indians and Asians, and a number of commentators have seen this as significant. Wherever the truth may lie, the reasons for the very different school performances of Asians and West Indians seem likely to lie deep within their respective cultures. It should also be said that the British school system has perceived the needs of these different groups of children rather differently.'[1]

PART 2

THE RESEARCH PROGRAMME

Background to the Research

i. The Crisis Comes to Light

It was in 1969, in a lengthy report specially commissioned by the Institute of Race Relations, that the attention of the general public was first drawn to the sorry predicament of Westindian schoolchildren in the UK. By that year the number of these children who were actually British-born was significant enough for there to be no more empty talk of 'purely transitional problems'. The report stated quite unequivocally:

> Children of West Indian parents, the largest of all immigrant groups [in Britain], have been a source of bafflement, embarrassment and despair in the educational system. They have complicated the attempts to define the term "immigrant pupil" and to assess the linguistic needs of immigrant pupils; in class, they have often presented problems which the average teacher is not equipped to understand, let alone overcome.[2]

It then proceeded to identify some of the special difficulties faced by Westindian pupils:

> [For some] there is first of all . . . an unexpected linguistic barrier when they first enter school; they cannot follow the teacher, nor make themselves understood . . .
>
> Secondly, many of the problems the children have derive from economic circumstances . . .
>
> Thirdly, the children's parents may place a greater burden upon them than would the average British parent . . .
>
> Finally, there are the problems which . . . derive directly from teachers and the school system in Britain. There is the problem of prejudice, and of the effect of teachers' expectations upon the children's progress, regardless of their intelligence . . . The problems of discrimination and expressions of racial prejudice in the wider society must inevitably affect the relationships which can be formed in the classroom . . . [3]

A number of other important points made in this seminal work are worth quoting here. For example:

> The quality which emerges most strongly from any account of the difficulties of Caribbean pupils is that of frustration . . . The children are in danger of losing confidence in themselves, and feeling that they have failed their parents; or they may

want to demonstrate their worth, but be unable to do so in terms which either their parents or their teachers understand or approve of. To complicate matters, their teachers and their parents are likely to ask different things of them.

Few West Indian children have been included in the more specialized language classes developed by some authorities. The justification for placing children in remedial classes . . . is that in a good class there will be small-group work, and plenty of individual attention. This can also be said of some special schools for ESN children, in which a disproportionate number of West Indian children are placed. ". . . migrant children, especially West Indians, admitted to ESN schools, may well have intellectual potential above the level of their assessed IQ . . ." (the last sentence is quoted from a report by the Inner London Education Authority).[4]

Thus some of the major problems of Westindian children in the UK were identified, if not probed into at the deepest level, in an influential report published as long ago as 1969. About three years later (it has not been possible to ascertain the exact date) an even more disturbing piece of writing, an article by respected journalist Colin Glashan, appeared in *The Observer*. This was the bleak opening paragraph:

If there is one thing that a 3,500-mile tour of young Black England has made clear for me, it is that this country is facing a racial crisis. Disaster may be a generation away, yet we are now near the point of no return. The patterns that are taking shape will be difficult, perhaps impossible to change. The equation is simple: in a democratic and affluent society, any visible minority that is denied dignity, self-respect and a viable family life is going to tear that society apart.[5]

The reader might well have expected the article to proceed along the well-known lines of Enoch Powell. But the author, rather than negatively pursue the 'rivers of blood' theme, analysed and illuminated the problems of young Westindians in a manner that has rarely, if ever, been equalled. 'Much of what's going wrong is in the schools,' he wrote, underlining the point with a harrowing illustration from a Birmingham school:

It is, irrationally, painful that the children look so healthy, so normal. They are sitting on a row of five chairs against the wall. The only other furniture is a mattress. The door is locked. The teacher, John, stands six feet in front of them, rustling a bag of crisps in his left hand. He calls their names loudly, one at a time. As each child stands up and walks hesitantly towards him, he thrusts out his right hand, palm upwards, and shouts "Hand!" Four of the children stick out a hand, receive some crisps and walk back to their chairs. The fifth, built like a weightlifter and named after one of the heroes of the British Empire, can't make it. At last, still sitting down, he wiggles his chair forward.

They are all boys aged 8—11, the eldest sons of Westindian immigrants, born in England. It has taken them nine months to get this far. None can speak. They only respond to their names and a few one-word commands. They have no sense of identity. They do not fit any recognised category and the staff have to struggle to define them for me. "Non-communicating hyperactive children with some psychotic and autistic characteristics," says the Headmaster finally. "I've seen white children like this, but they are very few and far between." A sixth of the children in the SSN (severely sub-normal) department of this school are boys like these, and their numbers are growing.

"Sub-normal" is a misleading label. These children are not the product of defective genes, disease, malnutrition or bangs on the head. They appear to be the result of the environment of slum housing and the child minder, of parents working long hours and crushed by unbearable problems and pressures. Whatever the reason, they're a new phenomenon. According to John, psychiatrists with experience in the West Indies have never seen them there. "I don't think there have been children like this before. I've been looking very hard into the literature and I can find nothing. The physical causation might be society itself."

The Headmaster talks of the children "corroded by society like a piece of iron." He has been sixteen years in the area. "We used to have very stable Westindian children at first. Now half the Westindian children in the SSN department are disturbed and speechless." He has a graph of their incidence by age groups. The lines for the total Westindian children and those disturbed rise at a steady 45-degree angle as they get younger. A footnote describes the implications as "urgent and serious".[6]

Finally, some comments from the same author on the British education system in general, and its effect upon Westindian children:

Going round the country, visiting school after school, one sees the same pattern: one or two black children in the top stream, one or two white children in the bottom. Either they are stupid, or the schools think they are stupid: it amounts to the same thing. Some schools are exceptions: there are teachers who care and understand. Overall, though, schools and teachers reflect society's assumptions. Subtly, unconsciously, and with the best of intentions, they are processing a generation of black children into an acceptance of inferiority. At best, their plight resembles that of the bright handicapped child, who is far too often expected to be content with a future making baskets; at worst,they inhabit a brutally unequal and second-rate system of education.[7]

ii. Rampton/Swann: the Underachievement of a Committee of Inquiry

In 1977 the Government's Select Committee on Race Relations and Immigration published a white paper entitled *The West Indian Community*. This reaffirmed that all the evidence indeed showed Westindians to be faring far worse at school than other children, and recommended that the matter should be the subject of a special inquiry. A year later a committee was set up by the Government to inquire into the education of children from ethnic minority groups, with particular reference to the underachievement of Westindian children, under the chairmanship of Anthony Rampton, OBE. The latter presided over an interim report, dealing exclusively with Westindian children, before handing over the chairmanship of the Committee to Lord Swann.

The interim report appeared in 1981 under the revealing title of *West Indian children in our schools*; the 'our' was a remarkable gaffe, bearing in mind that the Committee clearly cites 'racism, both intentional and unintentional'[8] as the primary factor in any consideration of the causes of underachievement. Not surprisingly, this issue is the least satisfactorily addressed in the report,* a tame piece of writing which nevertheless provides even more conclusive evidence of the appalling predicament of Westindian schoolchildren:

> While we accept that there will perhaps always be some children who will underachieve and for various reasons will fail to reach their full potential, our concern is that Westindian children *as a group* are underachieving in our education system.[9]

Apart from racism, the report identifies several other factors contributing to underachievement. These include 'the inadequacy of pre-school provision', 'the particular linguistic difficulties of West Indian children', 'the inappropriateness of the curriculum and the examinations system', 'teachers' low expectations of West Indian pupils', and 'a loss of trust and a lack of understanding between teachers and West Indian parents'. To these are added the wider factors (i.e., the effects are more obvious outside than inside schools) of 'the general state of race relations, discrimination in employment, conflict with authority figures, notably the police, and the relative absence of West Indians in prominent positions of responsibility in society who could be seen as "role models" for young West Indians.'[10]

Four years after the interim report the Committee, now under the chairmanship of Lord Swann, published its complete findings in *Education for All*, a massive volume about seven times as large (and seven times as great a disappointment) as the Rampton document. As far as Westindians are concerned, Swann's results are little advance on Rampton; this despite the fact that one of the express purposes of the interim report was to highlight matters which could then be dealt with fully in the final report. It repeats the Committee's firm conviction that

* An abridged version of Caribbean House's response to the report, written shortly after its publication, may be found in Appendix B at the end of this volume.

'Westindian children, as a group, and on average, are underachieving, both by comparison with their school fellows in the White majority, as well as in terms of their potential',[11] but in no way does it succeed in transcending the superficiality of the interim report in its analysis or – more inexcusably still – its recommendations.

The remarks concerning racism are amplified to the extent of acknowledging the many guises in which racism can appear, whether blatant, covert or unwitting. The issue of institutional racism and the general climate of racism in Britain are addressed as follows:

We believe that institutional racism is just as much a cause for concern as the prejudiced attitudes which some individuals may hold, since the establishment, in this way, of racism within the "system" itself can serve to reinforce, to magnify and to perpetuate such attitudes even where individual attitudes may be open to change . . .[12]

In considering the influence which racism whether intentional or unintentional can have on the education process we feel that it is essential to recognise the very direct and acute bearing which the general "climate" of racism in this country has on what takes place in the classroom.[13]

Recommendations as to how racism can be effectively tackled are, however, conspicuous by their absence. A typically vague if well-meaning conclusion, appearing in various forms of wording in different parts of the book, is that

. . . we should do all we can to diminish prejudice and discrimination within the educational system, and, through the next generation, outside it; and, simultaneously, we should give every help and encouragement within the educational system to enable minority children to overcome their disadvantages.'[14]

The issue of racism, at both institutional and individual level, should be considered openly and efforts made to counter it.[15]

It is necessary to combat racism, to attack inherited myths and stereotypes, and the ways in which they are embodied in institutional practices.[16]

The issue of racism need not be dwelt on here as it is looked at in more depth elsewhere in this book. Nor is it necessary to consider the Rampton/Swann Reports in greater detail. This brief glimpse at their contents does, however, serve a valuable twofold purpose in this context. It shows that the under-achievement of Westindian children in British schools is an officially established fact (and that there is an awareness of many contributory factors if not, perhaps, the ability or genuine determination to eradicate them); and it is a striking demonstration of the impotence and incongruity of mainstream inquiries into minority concerns beyond those embraced by the Establishment. Even the efforts of Lord Scarman, who won many friends among the Westindian community when he headed the inquiry into the Brixton riots of 1981, could not overcome this monumental hurdle.

The Rampton Report was published after Westindian Concern had begun the research project which is the subject of this book; the Swann Report appeared long after the project was completed. What these Reports succeeded in doing was to underline the need for an approach such as we adopted, with a practical methodology designed to produce the most accurate possible results. We venture to suggest that no-one other than a Westindian could have achieved this, and that our findings are as close as anyone will ever get to the reality of the situation.

The Testimony of Four Young Westindians

Westindian Concern (Caribbean House) was one of several Afro-Caribbean organisations invited to submit evidence to the Rampton Committee of Inquiry. This was done, as it turned out, shortly after the training phase of the research programme had begun. The text of our own evidence, which included the documentary film referred to on p. 108, was subsequently published in booklet form by the Centre for Caribbean Studies under the title *The Eye of the Storm*. More significantly in this context, four of our trainee research workers also gave evidence in the form of answers to questions about their background and experiences. These experiences were what helped them later to establish a rapport with the subjects of our research, and we had a number of built-in safeguards to ensure that this did not prejudice the interviews they conducted. It should also be noted that their answers to the Committee's questions were entirely truthful, which they needed to be not only from a moral point of view but because of the rigorous scrutiny to which their shrewd and experienced interrogators subjected them. Their testimony, which is summarised below, speaks for itself.

Interview A: 20-year-old Jamaican female

'I came to Britain at the age of eight. My mother had gone there seven years earlier, leaving my grandmother to look after me. I cannot remember a great deal about my first day at school in Jamaica. I only know that I was able to read by the time I attended school at the age of five.*

At the first school I went to in Britain I was placed in the lowest stream of my age group. I was really way above the rest of my class, but I just could not talk to my teacher. I wanted to let her know that I had read *Janet and John* books before, that I knew them backwards. I can remember trying to say this to her and being told: "Please speak English". This made the other children laugh at me, which was very embarrassing. From then on I could hardly open my mouth for fear of being laughed at again. I began to play the fool and mess about rather than face being put in that position. I always had the greatest difficulty

* In Jamaica the official age for starting school is 6, but this girl was brighter than average.

understanding the teachers. When I asked them to repeat something I was told that I should pay more attention. I *had* been paying attention, but could not follow what was being said.

I could not talk to my mother about things. She thought everything that happened at school was my fault. She thought I was not trying hard enough. I liked going to school just to get away from her. I often cried and wished that I could go back to Jamaica.

At eleven I went to Catford County, where I spent the rest of my schooldays. But I did not take any school-leaving examinations. I had been able to read and write when I arrived in Britain at the age of eight, but by the time I left school at 16 I could hardly write my name.'

Interview B: 20-year-old Antiguan male

'I was born in Britain and brought up from the age of two by Jamaican foster parents after the death of both my mother and father. I attended Northwold Junior and Upton House School, both in Hackney. I saw school as an escape from the strict conditions at home. But at school I did not receive any support or understanding of the problems I was facing both at home and at school. Because I never got any pocket money, I began stealing at school. I also became disruptive in my efforts to attract attention, and at Upton House I was branded a "troublemaker".

In my early schooldays I always used to ask the teacher twice what she said, because although I had heard quite well I did not understand what she meant. In the end I gave up trying to ask her and pretended I had understood. I would then ask a friend sitting nearby to explain it to me, but the teacher would say: "Stop talking and pay attention!" I would often cry when this happened. Gradually I fell way behind the rest of my age group and assumed that I was backward.

The best thing that ever happened to me was when I went to Jamaica to finish my education. Even though I found it all very strange and new, I had no difficulty understanding the teachers there. In fact my first teacher took a personal interest in me and helped me not only to correct my behaviour but eventually to catch up with the rest of my class.'

Interview C: 19-year-old Jamaican female

'I was born in Birmingham, but at the age of eight my mother sent me to live with my grandmother in Jamaica. I thought I had been doing all right at primary school in Handsworth, and the strangeness of the teacher's way of talking was something I had taken for granted, but when I went to school in Jamaica I discovered I was very backward. I had to be put in the lowest class with kids who were two or even three years younger than me. Teachers expected better of me because I had come from England, but compared to the others I was a dunce.

I felt very ashamed of myself, but they showed interest in me and I understood them in the same way I understood my mother. I could communicate with them easily. I had seven 'O' levels by the age of sixteen. But my aunt's children in Birmingham, who are about my age and went to the same school as I did in Handsworth, have not even got one 'O' level between them.'

Interview D: 19-year-old Jamaican male

'My father came to work in Britain shortly before I was born and my mother joined him not long afterwards, leaving me in the care of my grandmother in Jamaica. I was doing very well at school when my parents decided to bring me over to England at the age of thirteen. I found schools here completely different. The first thing I noticed was a lack of respect both for teachers and for school property. Also there was not the relationship between teacher and pupil to which I had been accustomed.

I had great difficulty following the teachers, and I put this down to their accents. But I was afraid to admit that I could not understand them. In the end I relied on text-books rather than any oral input from teachers. I do not know what would have happened had I not been able to read fluently when I entered the British school system. I was very ambitious then, but when I left school I had no 'O' Levels and had lost all desire to further my education.'

Methodology

In undertaking a research project of this kind, the first problem to be solved is that of authenticity: how to obtain reliable information from a community of people who are basically very reluctant to divulge anything about themselves, especially that which they perceive as being unfavourable to them. For historical and other reasons Westindians as a group have a strong desire, be it conscious or unconscious, to present inaccurate pictures of themselves or to distort information in order to show themselves up in a good light.

Traditional survey methods were therefore clearly of no use to us, since there was more than a possibility that the data thus collected could be falsified. Our best hope of obtaining genuine results was to carry out an action-research investigation employing non-survey techniques. This we did by using not only three separate profiles – individual, family, and school (or place of work) – but three distinct means: observation and active involvement, physical evidence, and documentary sources.

Interviews recorded on tape formed the main part of the observation/involvement. The interviewers were observers sharing in the lives and activities of their subjects, taking careful note of everything going on around them, unobtrusively recording conversation whenever possible and supplementing it with any available physical and documentary evidence. The observation extended also to the interviewers themselves, whose reaction to problems and interaction with each other, as well as their general approach and conduct, were kept under constant scrutiny. Identifiable areas of anxiety or need were referred by them to the family-centred child-care service at Caribbean House (see Appendix A), providing a further source of valuable extra information, albeit even more confidential.

Physical evidence was often found in data not gathered specifically for research purposes but nonetheless exploitable for those ends. Such evidence might include items of note in the home, housing conditions, relationships within the family, or observable characteristics of the interviewees or their parents. The major advantage of this kind of evidence is that it is basically objective in character, and can be secured without the subject knowing that it will be used for research purposes.

Documentary evidence was also obtained by the interviewers in the form of letters, written records and photographs. These proved of value in verifying the accuracy of certain statements made by the interviewees. In some cases we pursued such evidence to the Caribbean itself and visited many of the places which had been spoken about. All in all the follow-up evidence which we acquired by these and other means gave us a fair idea of the reliability of an interviewee's recall regarding experiences either here or in the West Indies.

The Myth of Objectivity

Social scientists such as Cherns, Rex, Gouldner, Mills and other critics of standard contemporary thinking in the field (and in sociology in particular) believe it is both inappropriate and misleading to apply the disciplines of natural science to research in the social sciences, an all too common practice among accredited social researchers. The reasons for the assumption of this borrowed structure lie, the critics point out, in the fact that it invests the social sciences with a respectability and supposedly value-free quality enabling them to claim parity with the natural sciences and to secure an established place in the academic world.

This is not to dispute the ideal of objectivity, which must always be at the heart of science. The questionable element lies in the adoption of a form of objectivity – in fact a pseudo-objectivity – which excludes anything that could possibly be construed as 'unscientific', ie anything that might produce results other than those which the social scientists wish to find.

This action-research investigation, however, is purely concerned with seeking an insight into and a genuine understanding of crucial social issues. In seeking a solution to a practical problem by getting to the source itself, it simply could not afford to be hampered or dictated by feudal arrangements between academics. Strenuous efforts were therefore made to maintain a balance between purely behavioural investigation on the one hand and investigation of the attitudes of a group which is basically unsusceptible to traditional approaches on the other. As such it can justly claim to be a major innovative contribution to research.

Selection and Training of Interviewers

An essential aspect of the research programme, perhaps the most crucial element of all, was that the interviewers were drawn from the same ethnic, linguistic and socio-economic group as those they were to interview, and had therefore all experienced much the same problems. They alone would make sense of what might seem unintelligible to others.

It was in the area of communication that most difficulties were anticipated, and it was here that our chosen policy paid off especially handsomely. How does one begin to communicate with young people who seem to be indifferent to what is going on around them, impervious to the approaches of outsiders, and operating in a cultural, linguistic and moral register all their own? It is so easy to assume that being English-speaking endows them with the same conceptual system as other native speakers of English. All the indications are, however, that they actually receive and understand things in a markedly different way to the rest of us, for even parents and other adults close to them virtually despair of reaching or communicating with these young people.

It was therefore necessary, if one was to get at the truth, to conceive a means of 'tuning in' to the subjects of our investigation. The only possible way of achieving this was to find and train interviewers from their own peer group, with whom they would share a common register in every sense. The rapport would be in many cases enhanced by the fact that, in accordance with the requirements of the project's sponsors, our interviewers were to be drawn from the ranks of the unemployed.

Selecting the interviewers was no easy task. Eight young people were chosen, six of them being of full Afro-Caribbean parentage and two the product of mixed marriages (English mother and Westindian father).* We could not be sure how long it would take to build an understanding between ourselves and the team, two of whom were to act as supervisors, so that everyone involved would be aware of exactly what was required. They obviously had to be given a thorough grounding in subjects of relevance to the research, as well as

* These two experienced noticeable difficulties in relating to the cultural and linguistic patterns of the others, but their greater eye for detail brought an excellent balance to the team.

specialised training in interviewing techniques that would enable them to tease out the information we required. In the event it was decided that an initial period of three months should be devoted to the training process.

The first four weeks were given over to input of the knowledge and the skills necessary to understand and relate to the present social, political, economic and industrial structure of our society. The purpose of this was to broaden the perspective and stimulate the confidence of the interviewers, who were all young and inexperienced. They first of all needed to be given assurance and a feeling of self-worth. To begin with it was as if they did not feel a part of their environment, but saw the world as hostile. The best way of countering this was to allow them some direct contact and interaction with some of the people who run Britain's institutions. This would not only present them with a unique learning opportunity, but would also enable them to see that society is run by ordinary people. A number of noted figures in public life, both local and national, made a valuable contribution to the training programme in this way, giving illuminating talks about their work and allowing the young people to question them at some length. All of them were courteous and patient, and some gave up as much as a whole day to share their experiences with the young trainees. There were occasional difficulties in communication, but these were soon rectified as we were able to make both sides aware that there were conceptual linguistic differences between them, and a skilled job in translating between Westindian patois and Standard English was carried out by the supervisors acting as interpreters. In this way a good rapport was established between these key establishment figures and the trainee interviewers.

The range of subjects covered was considerable. Mark Bonham Carter described the workings of the BBC, Bishop Guazelli discussed the role of the Catholic Church, David Bamber and Alan MacFarlane talked about local authority mechanisms (particularly in Hackney), and Ronald Howell went into the work of a juvenile court. From the world of politics, Lord Longford talked about how the House of Lords operates, Clinton Davis about the House of Commons and the Labour Party, and Andrew Rowe about the Conservative Party. Hal Austin looked at the Black media and their problems, Mary Sugden described the operations of Hackney Social

Services, and Daphne Stewart covered the work of Careers Offices. The names of the other contributors, no less important than those given here, are listed in the acknowledgements at the beginning of this book.

One name, however, must be singled out for special mention. Commander David Mitchell of the Metropolitan Police did much to explain the work of the police and went into the many problems in an admirably candid manner. Fear of the police, with real or imaginary justification, was discernible in all these young people, but after the session with Commander Mitchell their feelings of hostility were appreciably reduced. They were not necessarily any happier about the way the police went about their business, but were able to face up to the ethnocentric base of police operations. They were also able to accept that this ethnocentricity was not confined to the police alone, being part of the structure of institutional racism. This helped them to recognize that anger and bitterness towards the police must be replaced with rational awareness of the need for politeness and cooperation if they wished to move about freely in gathering information. Much good came of this direct contact with the police, with dialogue and communication largely dispelling fear, confusion and hostility. It was a pity that Commander Mitchell was soon afterwards transferred to another area, a move which – with all due respect to his successor – effectively prevented us from building on this promising beginning.

As every one of the youngsters went on to both educational and career achievements, the part these public figures played in altering the course of their lives cannot be underestimated. The central point was that trainee interviewers needed to understand that the work on which they were embarking was in its way as important as anything that these dignitaries were doing, and they needed to see themselves in that light. Very little would be achieved if they were to go around feeling worthless and uncertain as they knocked on the doors and tried to talk to their interviewees. They had to feel that they were making a contribution to society. It was therefore continually stressed that the task in which they were engaged was one that nobody but themselves could do, and that none of the public figures with whom they came into contact during the three months of training was equipped to carry out that task.

Interviewing Young Westindians

Training in specialised interviewing techniques was crucial to the research, not least because the interviewers faced the task of having to operate in many different registers or ways of communicating and being understood and accepted. In other words, the register they would use for children would not be the same as for parents, and this again would differ markedly from the register they would use for the wider public. If they were to be well received among Westindians they had to be careful to say nothing that might cause offence or frighten people off. Use of the word 'research', for instance, was discouraged because it gave the impression of singling individuals out for questioning or placing them under the spotlight; and Westindians, young and old alike, do not like being asked searching questions under any conditions, let alone being placed under the spotlight.

The reasons for this state of affairs are not hard to see. The fact is that, consciously or unconsciously, whatever their pretence might be, most Westindians are not very proud of their situation. Their lack of security is so great that they feel they have more to hide than most people, and for them to volunteer certain things about themselves, especially to people they hardly know and with whom they have no relationship, would be like tearing their guts out. So it would be quite futile to turn up on their doorsteps and say: 'I've come to see you because I'm doing a bit of research, and we think you can help us'.

Initially it was suggested that the interviewers should adopt a quasi-casual approach, knocking on doors and engaging those who answered – usually parents – in friendly conversation. In the course of this they were to mention in a matter-of-fact way that they were carrying out an investigation or an inquiry to find out whether or not Black children were getting their due at school or at work – and the only way of doing this was to check it out with the Black kids themselves. The interviewers could truthfully say that they had their own experience of schools in this country – and some in the West Indies as well – which they wanted to compare with others who had gone through or were still part of the school system here. They could equally say, in all honesty, that they saw no reason why there should not be more lawyers and doctors and other top professionals among Black people, and indeed why this should not include the children of those whom they had engaged in conversation.

If parents said they were satisfied that their children were being treated all right at school, that in itself was important, and interviewers would emphasise that this too needed to be checked out with the youngsters themselves; it would be good to know that some Westindian children are happy with things as they are. Conversely, if parents were not satisfied with the way their child was performing at school, that would also be a good enough entrée. This approach, although it was in fact abandoned in favour of a letter taken home by children (see p. 55), is a good example of operating in the parents' register.

Once inside there would be a subtle shift of register in the direction of the children. Parents would almost invariably keep an eye on the opening gambit and stay around until they felt they could trust the interviewer with their little lambs. Because of this, the best kind of question to start off with would be about what the youngsters' favourite subjects were, and whether they were getting all the help they needed in those subjects at school. They, like their parents, needed to understand that it was *their* story we wanted, whatever it was, and that as such it was nothing to be ashamed of. It was also stressed that instead of writing it down the interviewer wanted to put it on tape, so as to be able to listen afterwards to how the talk went. Participants would have the chance to join in hearing the playback if they wished, and anything they did not like would be deleted.

Interviewees were asked to produce school reports, and if they agreed to do so these would be read aloud with them so that they formed part of the taped material. The chief value of the reports lay in the many questions that naturally arose out of them: what the interviewees thought this or that comment by a teacher meant, and so on. Without prejudicing the answers, interviewers might well feign a stance of hostility towards the teachers so that the subjects would not feel they were being put in the dock. This sympathetic approach was one which generally encouraged individuals to be much more forthcoming about their attitudes than they might otherwise have been.

Because Westindians, perhaps uniquely, regard the word 'no' as hostile and will seldom use it unless they feel in a hostile mood, it was necessary to avoid asking questions to which that might be the answer – or to ask questions in such a way that no one-word answer would suffice. The need for this, and for the feigned hostility towards teachers, is in itself indicative of the sickness which afflicts the Westindian community and which gave rise to this research project. The use of such techniques, no doubt unheard of among social scientists, is what we may term 'social engineering'; judiciously applied, it is the only way to get at the truth among Westindians.

Social engineering is best illustrated by the example of a Westindian mother who is very old-fashioned in her dealings with her daughter. The latter is a bit of a tearaway, though perhaps no worse than most other teenage girls, but her mother has broken up with the girl's father and badly wants to show him that she can be mother, father and everything combined to her children. She is therefore determined, by hook or by crook, even by force if necessary, that her daughter is going to be a 'good girl' and not let her down. But she works so hard at it that she is in danger of cracking up under the strain. An astute caseworker called in to deal with this situation will quickly recognise that the problem lies not with the girl but with the mother, and will not say that the girl is behaving badly, even if the mother is saying so and it is obviously true. To agree with the mother's assertions here would be disastrous; she must be continually bolstered and reassured about what a nice daughter she has, so that she feels she is doing a good job.

That is social engineering. It is helping the mother, and very probably helping the daughter in turn (part of the exercise, of course, is to get the girl to behave better). But as Rome was not built in a day, so nobody can be a tearaway one minute and an angel the next. If the mother is over-anxious, the caseworker is not going to have the kind of breathing space needed in these circumstances in order to work things out.

If, therefore, you are questioning young Westindians on the touchy subject of their attitudes or performance at school, you must use social engineering if you are to elicit a truthful response and avoid having a disturbing effect on the household. It is part of the European mentality that people must want to do things or give their consent to an offer of help if anything is to be done for them. This is not the case with Westindians, who have to be engineered into receiving help because they will seldom acknowledge that they need it. By the same token they have to be manoeuvred into divulging information about themselves, which is something they would otherwise be most unlikely to do, regardless of the benefits.

Many Westindian children have themselves become very adept at social engineering of a more dubious kind. They have developed almost to perfection the art of playing off one parent against another and of manipulating social workers and others for their own ends. They end up in government institutions, where it costs the taxpayer two or three hundred pounds a week to maintain them without anyone, least of all the youngsters themselves, gaining anything from the exercise. In dealing with that sort of mentality it becomes a question of 'out-engineering' the individuals concerned. It is engineer versus engineer, the one living from day to day entirely on his wits, with immediate and limited objectives that are quite predictable, and the other thinking and planning ahead with cool rationality.

The most important thing from the interviewer's point of view, however, was to ensure that the conversation would not dry up completely before it had really begun. The success of an interview clearly depended a great deal on the interviewers themselves. The more skilled the interviewer, the less likely there was to be a complete breakdown in communication. The best way of breaking down barriers is to make friends with people, but this on its own would have been insufficient here without the back-up of particular skills – for example, the adroit and unobtrusive use of tape machines, the ability to record anything at the flick of a finger without giving the impression of 'setting things up'.

Over the years we ourselves have had to deal with a number of very difficult young people, many of whom are now doing responsible jobs in all walks of life. Some, when we first came into contact with them, were non-communicative, surly, hostile, and even vicious. Trying to sit down with them and arrive at some kind of meeting point was almost impossible. One way of getting round this was to ask these young people to assist us in the work we were doing. They might be suspicious at first, but gradually they would respond and try to help. But when they came up against people like themselves, they would be the first to come to us and say: Why do you bother with him? He's no good, he's useless, man!' The discussions that would follow frequently contained some of the most valuable lessons that these newly reformed characters would ever learn.

Guidelines and Code of Conduct for Interviewers

In addition to the formal list of questions, which had to be more or less memorised, interviewers were issued with the list of guidelines given below. This was so that they would have something to which they could refer without difficulty when out in the field.

Main questions about school

- Curriculum content.
- Teacher/pupil relationships and attitudes to each other.
- Achievement.
- Peer group influence.

Main questions about home

- Who do you live/stay with?
- Who did you grow up with?
- Tell me something about yourself.
- Supplementary questions arising out of answers given (allow interviewees to introduce remarks about the family during general talk about themselves if possible).

Golden rules

- Do not create a barrier.
- Listen very carefully, and do not go over ground that has already been covered.
- Ask things in a way that does not seem like a question, otherwise people are liable to clam up.
- Create a relaxing influence and be sympathetic and friendly.
- Have safe questions easily to hand in case of trouble.
- Emphasise total confidentiality, i.e., no names used.
- Introduce tape recorder as being needed for the benefit of the interviewer.
- Do not pursue a delicate question – watch for signals, and if a question sparks off discomfort, leave it alone (bring it up later if this can be done without problems).
- Make interviews as spontaneous as possible, e.g., at street corners.
- No salesmanship or fast talk.

- Don't look over-confident.
- Play down the interviewer/interviewee roles; make it casual and chatty.
- Never be pushy.
- Don't make out you are doing anyone any favours.

Problem: Interviewee refuses to be taped

1. Grasp full implications.
2. If bright, give a reason for tape (people speak faster than you can write, you can't do shorthand, importance of getting their views across correctly).
3. If not bright, find other forms of persuasion according to the situation.
4. If necessary, make a good break (e.g., I'm going to eat – want to come?).
5. Remember the tape recorder is a common and not an alien phenomenon.

Approach

- Show sympathy and empathise with interviewee.
- Everything is personal, confidential, private.
- 'I want to get to know you,' not 'Answer my questions.'
- Show interest by drawing them on their interests.

General points

- Make your own contacts, especially in clubs and the like.
- Develop your own line of conversation.
- Bring in your own experience.
- Encourage interviewees to express their own personal views.
- Maintain seriousness.
- We want results, not mere talk.
- Remember tendency of Westindians to give conditioned answers or half-truths. Persuade them that real answers have more value.

Interview Summary

1. How did the interviewee come over?
2. How difficult were they (i.e., the individual) to see?
3. Were they articulate?
4. Do you think they were honest?
5. What made you think so?

6. How many times did you see them?
7. Which subjects were they willing to talk about?
8. What subject did they seem unwilling to talk about?
9. Did you discover the reason why?
10. How did they answer on the most sensitive subjects in the profile?
11. Did they find English difficult?
12. Did they understand all you were talking about?
13. How often did you have to repeat your questions?
14. Do you feel that they said they understood but did not really?
15. What made you think so?
16. How did they react to what you were doing?
17. How did they respond to being recorded?

CODE OF CONDUCT

The following served as a job description as well as a list of rules governing the discipline and conduct of interviewers:

1. Interviewers will be required to meet members of the general public as an integral part of their duties. In the exercise of such duties they must extend courtesy to all members of the public even under difficult and trying circumstances.

2. Interviewers will be required to make contact with young Blacks, primarily between the ages of 14 and 20. Such contact shall be for the purposes of gathering specific information, using audio-interviewing techniques that the interviewer will have developed and acquired through Westindian Concern's training programme.

3. Every interview must be treated as highly confidential, as must every matter externally or internally connected with this project.

4. The management shall reserve the right to take legal action against, or to dismiss instantly and without pay, anyone committing a breach of such confidentiality. Any sums due shall be deposited with the company's solicitors pending the outcome of legal proceedings. If legal proceedings are not initiated within one month of dismissal, all sums due to a former worker up to the time of dismissal must be paid to him or her.

5. All initial contacts shall first be made in Hackney, after which research workers will be expected to travel within and beyond Hackney in order to maintain such contacts.
6. No more than 10 hours should be given over to any one client, but this may be spread over as many days as are necessary.
7. Decisions about where to travel and whom to see shall rest with the supervisors, by whom any initiative must be sanctioned.
8. Care must be taken of recorders and tapes, which shall remain the property of Westindian Concern at all times, and must not be loaned to anyone not connected with the project.
9. Tapes shall be handed in daily and documented in the prescribed manner.
10. The co-ordinator and the supervisors shall comprise the disciplinary board which will deal with any breach of the rules.
11. During the 12-week training period a trainee may be instantly dismissed for any of the following reasons:
    - being late by 30 minutes or more on more than three occasions without an excuse that is satisfactory to supervisory staff;
    - absence for a day or more, except when due to illness or other acceptable excuse (a telephone call notifying the office of illness must be received no later than one hour after work was due to begin, and a doctor's certificate must be obtained if absence is for more than three days);
    - refusal to carry out a direction from a supervisor;
    - stealing or threatening behaviour towards any member of the public.
12. During the training period a trainee who is more than an hour late for work or who fails altogether to report for work, without prior assent or reasonable excuse in the eyes of supervisory staff, shall be liable to a reduction in pay of £10 per day (the equivalent of one day's pay).

Obstacles and Difficulties

In attempting a research project of this nature it was perhaps inevitable that we should run up against many obstacles, some of them considerable, some quite unforeseen. Even before it got underway there was what appeared to be an insoluble problem, that of devising an entirely new methodology differing in almost every way from the traditional questionnaire approach. As far back as 1976 we had looked into the possibility of enrolment on a special course in survey research methods run by the Survey Unit at the Social Science Research Council, only to be told that what one would learn there was quite unsuited to the nature of our proposed investigation.

Once we had formulated a potentially workable scheme, i.e., one that was both tailored to the particular demands of the subject and likely to attract the necessary funding, we set about the task of finding sponsors. Our first port of call was the Inner London Education Authority, followed soon afterwards by the London Borough of Hackney; although both expressed interest, neither felt able to finance the research. However, the latter did at least agree to provide badly needed grant-in-aid for the Family Casework Unit at Caribbean House, and this it has done without interruption since 1978. When we first approached the Special Programmes Division of the Manpower Services Commission about the project they, too, turned down our request for funds. But, eventually, at the beginning of 1980, they accepted it on the grounds that the interviewers would be drawn from the ranks of the long-term unemployed.

The only drawback of the MSC funding, which came to around £80,000, was that it did not meet the full scale of the project we had in mind and, therefore, additional sponsors had to be sought. We tried a number of Trusts – including Gulbenkian, Sainsbury, Hilden, Trafalgar, Rowntree and Queen's Silver Jubilee – without success. We also sent grant applications to MIND (the National Association for Mental Health) and to the Mental Health Foundation, both of whom were unable to help because they felt our scheme could not really be classified as a mental health project. It was nevertheless encouraging to receive an enthusiastic letter from one of MIND's campaign organisers – David Brandon, an experienced researcher who had himself carried out a far-reaching investigation into matters affecting ethnic minorities

– expressing unqualified approval of our approach, which he described as 'the most appropriate method to provide the particular kind of balance for which you are seeking.'

Even with the smaller sample of 508 for which we eventually had to settle, there were many essential ingredients which required our finance to be doubled at least. Accordingly, we made strenuous attempts to secure the shortfall from the Department of Education and Science, the Department of the Environment, the Home Office, the ILEA, the Nuffield Foundation and the Commission for Racial Equality, all to no avail. So we started off and did what we could with the slender resources available to us and, in the end, we had to be content with the results of these efforts. The one small bit of extra funding we did receive came from the Methodist Church's Division of Social Responsibility, who kindly agreed to donate £400 to the project. Also, the acquisition of a mini-computer enabled us to organise and analyse the collected data in a far more efficient manner than had previously been envisaged.

Not surprisingly, although they responded well to their training, the interviewers encountered a number of problems out in the field. Firstly, as we had predicted, the unannounced appearance of complete strangers on their doorsteps did not go down very well with Westindians. I therefore sought the permission of the ILEA to approach children at school (especially those between the ages of 13 and 16) and enlist the cooperation of the schools concerned in contacting parents and contributing generally to the research. This permission was withheld for two reasons: firstly, they did not want us to interview Westindian children only and felt that we should extend our research to all teenage pupils, regardless of origin; and, secondly, they accused us of dishonesty in that the subjects would not know they were being observed for research purposes. In fact, all 508 interviewees were eventually told all about the research project in which they were taking part, but only after interviewers had established a rapport with them; they could then insist, if they wished, that we delete all the information they had given to us. In only one instance was this found to be necessary.

Because of the ILEA's intractable attitude, which included insistence on a number of additional constraints that might have hampered us, we decided to approach children outside the school gates. Interviewers handed them a letter to take home to their parents (see facing page), a policy which drew protests

CARIBBEAN HOUSE GROUP

INCORPORATING

MISSION TO THE WEST INDIANS IN BRITAIN

CARIBBEAN HOUSE
BRIDPORT PLACE
LONDON N1 5DS
Telephone 01-729 0986

Dear Parents,

Some Parents are not satisfied with the way their children are getting on at school. Some think that their children are doing all right but have no way of really knowing if this is true or not. One thing is certain – that is, that most black children can do much better than they are doing at present.

If you have a teenage child – by that we mean children in their teens, 13, 14, 15 up to 19, in school or who have left school, we would like your permission to meet with you and your child or children to talk about their schools, about the way they feel about things in this country and what they would like from life.

We are carrying out an investigation which we hope will result in helping your children to do better at school and to help them to obtain better jobs. This is a chance to really do something for black children. We would like to hear from the children themselves what they feel and what they think.

We have trained a team of young people to conduct this investigation, so if a young person turns up and say he or she is from Caribbean House or Westindian Concern ask for his/her identity. If you are satisfied that they are from us – please give them all the co-operation you can. Give us a ring if you wish to know more about all this. There is one thing you can be sure of – they will not lead your children astray.

Thanking you,

Ashton Gibson

from two head teachers. However, 452 out of 500 parents contacted in this way agreed to help us, and of these we were only able to take up 308. In fact, due in no small measure to our method of approach, the cooperation we received from parents in allowing and facilitating interviews with their adolescent children went far beyond our expectations.

The remaining 200 interviewees were in the 16–19 age bracket and were therefore approached in a different way altogether, often in clubs or cafes, on street corners, in amusement arcades, or at blues parties. This meant that some interviews had to be initiated at unsocial hours, but this was unavoidable if a wide cross-section of Westindian teenagers was to be tapped. It also gave rise to certain practical problems: occasionally the tape recorder picked up so many extraneous noises – cars, chatter, music, dishes, etc. – that the speaker was completely drowned out. Arrangements were therefore made to meet these people in their homes or somewhere quiet where they felt relaxed. In some cases the names they had given us turned out to be false. In others they were found to have lost interest between the initial approach and the home visit, but avoided confrontation by getting their parents to say that they (the children) did not wish to take part; very few actually stated this themselves. Some parents told us of their own accord that they did not want their children involved. Whenever such a rebuff occurred it obviously reflected on the interviewer, but as time went on it became apparent that there was a general apathy that had to be overcome.

Once interviews were underway the problem often lay in maintaining the subject's interest, a considerable challenge in many instances. Interviewers endeavoured to overcome this by turning the questions as much as possible into a conversation. Another frequent problem, especially with 13- or 14-year-olds, was the continuing presence of the mother or father in the room. In these circumstances, when matters such as the family or personal habits outside the house were touched on, children tended to give a wrong or modified answer because the truth might annoy their parents. The only way round this, if the latter persisted in remaining within earshot, was to arrange for the next interview to take place at a different location such as Caribbean House or a friend's home, or somewhere else where the youngster would feel comfortable. This particular problem was rarely encountered with older interviewees.

Full list of Questions

The full range of questions asked by the interviewers far exceeded that implied in the summary of assembled data, and spawned a wealth of information which helped us not only to clarify or substantiate answers to some of the most crucial questions, but also to understand more about the picture from an overall point of view. Some of these questions were purely 'bait', i.e., a way of introducing a touchy subject* indirectly or informally, with the aim of drawing out information which might not otherwise be forthcoming. Interviewers had more or less to memorise what they needed to ask in order to play down the 'questionnaire' aspect and prevent interviewees from feeling they were being interrogated.

Listed below are the questions put to school-leavers, including some aspects which we eventually had to telescope considerably because our limited funding compelled us to concentrate mainly on educational underachievement. Those still at school were asked almost all the same questions (i.e., excluding those about unemployment or the workplace) with the present tense substituted for the past where appropriate.

1. SCHOOL AND EDUCATION

a) Attitude towards school
- what did you think of school?
- how was it for you?
- did you like school?
- do you think the education system is fair?

b) Achievement
- (note scale:) University – Degree
  T.E.C. – Higher Diploma (HND)
  Diploma (HNC)
  Higher Cert. (OND)
  Certificate (ONC)
  School – GCE 'A' level
  – GCE 'O' level
  – CSE
  – Nil

* e.g., reports, truancy, suspension.

- did you do well at school?
- did you get as much out of school as you wanted?
- was school any good for you?
- did anyone have faith in you at school?
- did you get any encouragement?
- did you find school hard, soft, easy, boring?

c) Ambitions at school
- were you hoping to get anything from school?
- what did you hope to get out of school?
- what were your ambitions?
- what is your potential in your opinion?
- have you any real potential?

d) Curriculum content
- what was your favourite/worst subject at school?
- were there any subjects you wanted to do but couldn't?
- were you given a choice of subjects?
- what subjects did you have to do (i.e., compulsory)?
- did you learn anything from your lessons that has helped you?
- did you learn anything about yourself in history lessons?
- do you know anything about Westindians, your roots, etc.?

e) Teacher/pupil relationship
- did you like any of your teachers?
- what kind of relationship did you have with your teachers?
- did you clash/experience conflict with any teacher?
- did you find your teachers fair on the whole?
- did you understand your teachers?
- did you and your teacher speak the same language?
- did any teacher take a personal interest in you?

f) Peer group influences
- did you have any classmates or school friends?
- did you hang out with your friends at school a lot?
- how did the school see you as a group?
- were you popular at school?
- were you influential?
- what did you and your mates spend your time doing at school (apart from work)?

g) Family influences
- did your parents ever come into the school?
- did your parents know anything about you at school?
- did your parents approve of the school you went to?
- did your parents help you at all with school work?
- did your parents have any conflict with your school?

2. HOME AND FAMILY

a) Attitude towards parents in general
- who do you live with?
- what are your parents like?
- do you get on well with your parents?
- who do you get on best with?
- did you grow up with your parents?
- are your parents in this country?
- do you see your parents often?

b) Attitude towards individual parents
- how do you feel about your mum/dad?
- tell me something about your mum/dad?

c) Family structure
- do you come from a big family?
- have you a lot of relatives?
- how close are your relatives?
- do you keep in touch with the rest of the family?
- how much of your family lives together?

d) Economic status
- what kind of a place do you live in?
- do you live in a council (flat/house)?
- have you ever been back to the Caribbean, on holiday or otherwise?
- does your family own a car?
- what kind of job does your dad do?
- does your mum work?
- does anybody in your family own their own business?

e) Harmony/conflict
- how close is your family?
- do your parents give you room to move?

- does your mum allow you to rave/go mad/have fun?
- do you feel comfortable at home?
- do your parents go out?
- do you like being at home?
- why don't you live at home?
- do you see your mum/dad?
- do you get on well with your brothers and sisters?

f) Contact with the establishment
- have you or your family ever come into contact with the police?
- have you or your family ever come into contact with the social services?

3. EMPLOYMENT

a) Type of work
- how did you get your job?
- what is your job?
- how do you earn your living?
- tell me something about your job
- do you keep to the same type of job?

b) Difficulties
- what age did you leave school?
- have you had any difficulties settling into a job?
- how many jobs have you had since you left school?
- do you easily get bored with your job?
- are you a good time-keeper?

c) Job satisfaction
- do you enjoy your work?
- is your job interesting?
- is it the work you really want?
- do you force yourself to go to work?
- are you satisfied/do you feel happy with your work?

d) Ambitions and aims
- what goal have you set yourself to reach in life?
- are you an ambitious person?
- how have you set about doing what you want to do?
- what are your aims work-wise?
- do you feel you will fulfil your job ambitions?

- do you hope to achieve anything in your life?
- what's stopping you?
- have your ambitions changed as you've grown older?
- how did your ambitions come about?
- what contacts have you got to help you fulfil your ambitions?
- are your ambitions realistic?
- have you got very high hopes for yourself?

e) Actual work potential
- does your job offer you promotion?
- is the promotion it offers realistic?
- do you have a fair chance of promotion?
- does your job involve you in a lot of responsibility?
- do you want a lot of responsibilities?
- do you want responsibilities of any kind in your job?

f) Relationship with management
- what sort of relationship do you have with your boss?
- have you ever had a quarrel with your boss?
- do you get along with your boss?
- does your boss see you as a person?
- do you respect your boss?
- does your boss treat you fairly?
- is your boss reasonable?
- can you trust your boss?
- do you have too many bosses in your job?
- does your boss take a personal interest in his workers?

g) Relationship with workmates
- do you have a lot of workmates?
- do you fit in easily with your colleagues at work?
- have you ever lost a job through workmates?
- are any of your workmates personal friends?
- do you meet workmates outside of work?
- does it matter to you whether you work with Whites only/Blacks only/a mixture? (what do you prefer?)
- do you relate to your White workmates?
- does tension ever develop between White and Black employees where you work?
- have you personally ever had conflict with a colleague at work because of your colour?

4. UNEMPLOYMENT

- how long have you been unemployed?
- why do you think you are unemployed?
- how many interviews have you been to since your last job?
- when was your last interview?
- do you get fair treatment at interviews in your opinion?
- when was the last time you went to a jobcentre?
- are you registered with the careers office?
- how do you go about looking for a job?
- has anybody ever helped you to find or look for a job?
- what help have you received towards finding a job?
- what is stopping you from getting a job?
- do you like work?
- what work are you looking for?
- do you think you will get the job you want?
- how interested are you in getting a job?
- have your expectations of finding a job changed since you first became unemployed?
- do you sign on?

5. SOCIETY IN GENERAL

- how do you see the Black man in this country/society?
- how do you see your role as a Black man in this society?
- what is your attitude to this society as a young Black?
- do you find that this society treats most people fairly?
- do you find Westindians are given a fair deal?
- what are the reasons for Westindians being kept back?
- where do you think Westindians in this country go wrong or do you think that is not so?
- how do you see yourself: Black British, Black, Coloured, African, African descent, Westindian generally or identifying with specific island?
- how do you feel about other ethnic groups (e.g., Asians, Jews)?

6. PEER GROUP

- are you connected with any organisations?
- what clubs do you go to?
- do you ever go to a youth club?
- are there enough places for you to go to?
- are you a loner?

- do you rave?
- do you move with friends?
- do you move about a lot?
- do you identify with friends?
- have you any White friends?
- what sort of music do you listen to?
- do you drink?
- do you smoke?
- are you politically minded?
- is it true that we as Black youths prefer to be on the streets rather than at home, and if so, why?

PART 3

THE RESEARCH FINDINGS

Summary of Research Data

(Consideration was given to grouping percentages in small blocks under various headings. However, because of overlapping and ambiguity of classification, the results are simply listed as they emerged after being broken down.)

1. General attitude towards school

41% saw school as a social outlet
18% saw school as a means of escaping from strict conditions at home
25% associated school with learning and equipping them for work
21% saw school as a waste of time

2. General attitude towards teachers

92% of attitudes towards teachers were determined by what they felt to be the teachers' attitudes to them
67% had a negative attitude towards teachers because of their feeling (real or imaginary) that one or more teachers were prejudiced against them

3. General attitude towards teacher/pupil relationship

84% said they had a good relationship with one or other particular teacher
26% had a good teacher/pupil relationship with staff as a whole

4. Ability to communicate with teachers

6% fully understood teachers
79% understood most of the time but not always

5. Reasons for lack of comprehension

There was a marked tendency to switch off from listening to teachers with whom they did not have a good relationship. However –

14% did not speak the same language

6. *Difficulty in hearing/understanding* – Primary School

14% had had no such difficulty in primary school

7. *Repetition of questions* – Primary School

It was felt that primary school teachers usually repeated questions if asked to do so

8. *Asking for questions to be repeated*

60% asked teachers to repeat questions they had not understood
45% were frequently not enlightened by the teacher's answer although appearing to convey that they were

9. *Teachers' response when asked to repeat something*

It was generally felt that teachers did respond but often gave the impression that they thought the child was not paying attention, and this discouraged further questions

10. *Difficulty in hearing/understanding* – Secondary School

70% had such problems with some teachers
58% had occasional problems
48% had such problems generally

11. *Dialect*

90% did not admit to speaking Creole or patois or other form of English at school, but
56% admitted they spoke differently at home, and
36% said they spoke differently with friends

12. *Difficulty in understanding parents or friends*

None had any such difficulties

13. *Understanding teachers in the same way as parents or friends*

64% did not understand teachers in the same way
40% experienced a slight difference
24% experienced a lot of difference

14. Finding school and/or teachers strange

The feeling of strangeness was generally hard to define, e.g., 'It was different from home' or 'It wasn't strange but very different'

15. Favourite subjects

Answers were very mixed, but
42% included Art among their favourites

16. Worst subjects

Maths and Languages

17. Choice of subjects

All were given a choice of subjects to do at school, but only
7% of their selections were consistent with taking up a discipline at degree level

18. Determination of choice

Few felt they had any choice in reality, opting for convenience or what they believed they could master, without giving any real thought to their choice

19. Help with choices

98% were given no help at all in making their choice

20. Compulsory subjects

Everyone cited English and Maths as compulsory, but
42% added at least two other subjects, saying these were compulsory when in fact this was not the case

21. Subjects they would have liked to do but could not

Technological subjects

22. Why were they not able to choose these subjects?

The general feeling was that taking CSE denied them that choice, i.e., they seemed to regard taking CSE as a confirmation of lack of ability in certain subjects

23. Extra help with certain subjects

38% felt they would have benefited from extra help had it been available, and
32% would have liked some extra help

24. Problem areas in English

25% found difficulty in comprehending the written word

25. Attitude towards reading

95% said they liked reading

26. Serious or light reading

12% had read a book of 100 pages or longer in the preceding month
88% apparently confined their reading to comics and the like

27. Works by Shakespeare, Dickens, George Lamming or Selvon

10% had read one or more works by these authors (the two last-named being the most widely-read Westindian writers)

28. Learning about themselves at school

None admitted to learning anything about themselves or their parents at school

29. Learning about the West Indies

4% learned something about the West Indies at school

30. Learning about slavery

Less than 1% said they learned anything about slavery at school

31. Significance of slavery

98% did not associate slavery with their roots

32. Date of abolition of slavery

None knew when slavery was abolished

33. View of School Performance

70% said they got on well at school, though it transpired that by this many meant they got on well with their friends, not that they performed well in school work

34. Gregariousness

Less than 1% were loners

35. Popularity

95% thought they were popular with their friends
33% courted or lived out this popularity in the classroom

36. Influence on others

25% thought they had influence on others

37. Group or gang membership

67% said they were part of a group

38. Their view of the group

The group was generally seen as a form of cultural protection, i.e., enabling them to do things together which, if done individually, would leave them open to criticism from teachers

39. School view of the group

Those who belonged to a group felt that teachers seldom saw them and their friends as a group, but that those teachers who did so regarded them as trouble-makers

40. Group activities off the school premises

80% could give no structural pattern to time spent with the group, describing activities only as 'play'

41. Membership of youth clubs

62% did not belong to any youth club
30% belonged to local church youth groups
8% were members of ILEA youth clubs

42. Reason for not belonging to a youth club

Parents did not encourage it

43. Assessment of their own school reports

20% felt their school reports were good

44. Wording of school reports

75% disagreed both with grades and with teachers' comments

45. Reasons for disagreement

62% said, in so many words, that they felt teachers exercised some sort of prejudice against them
35% thought they were marked down deliberately
27% felt they were not liked by the teacher

46. Effect of school reports on parents

74% thought that a bad report soured their relationship with their parents, but that plaudits were unlikely to be forthcoming if a report was good

47. 5th-year examinations

The majority had taken or were going to take five or six CSEs, or thought they would take six or seven 'O' levels

48. 6th-form entry

71% of school-leavers did not enter the 6th form
2-3% of those who stayed on took 'A' levels

49. Reasons for not entering 6th-form

65% of school-leavers had felt nothing much was happening

50. 'O' and 'A' levels

Less than 2% had passed in five or more 'O' levels, and less than 1% had two 'A' levels

51. Truancy

89% had never played truant, but –
70% had skipped certain classes

52. Reasons for missing classes

65% said this was because they did not like the teacher concerned

53. Frequency of missed classes

The pattern varied from week to week

54. Being placed on report

50% said they had been placed on disciplinary reports, but the evidence suggests that half of them could be mistaken, i. e., they had only received a severe censure

55. Suspension from school

7% said they had been suspended from school, each of them on only one occasion

56. Length of suspension

A week or less was the term of suspension for half of the above, while the other half never returned to school

57. Reasons for suspension

75% of those who had been suspended gave class violence as the reason

58. Attitude to suspension

Those suspended would probably not return to school if given the choice. There was a resigned acceptance rather than any deep resentment of the verdict

59. Special schools or classes

Less than 5% had ever attended any type of special school or special classes

60. Special schools at primary or secondary school age

Less than 2% had attended a special school at normal school age

61. Feelings about being in a special school

None of those involved seemed to care, i.e., there was no feeling of stigma

62. Effect of special schools

Those involved did not appear to know whether such schools helped them in any way

63. Reasons for being sent to a special school

No-one really knew why they had been sent to a special school; most thought it was because they had been 'mucking about'

64. School visits by parents

81% of parents visited their child's school

65. Open day visits

Open day attendance by parents was good at primary school age, but as the children got older it tailed off and was generally poor at secondary school age

66. School visits other than on open days

50% of parents visited school at other times

67. Parents' knowledge of the school

60% thought parents only knew about the school from what they (the children) told them

68. Parents' view of the school

71% of parents did not approve of the secondary school attended by their child, but only
3% of parents said that the school was not their first choice

69. Parental help with school work

10% of parents helped their children with homework

70. Desired school-leaving age on entering secondary school

80% had wanted to leave school after the 6th year (i.e., at 18)

71. Desired school-leaving age at 3rd- and 4th-form level

70% wished to leave school after the 6th year

72. Actual school-leaving age

71% of those who had left did so at 16, and more than half of the remainder at 17, therefore a total of
85% left before the end of the 6th-form year

73. What school had to offer them

91% thought school offered qualifications for work through the passing of exams, although less than 2% had any exam passes to their credit

74. Earliest memories

70% were very vague, but 90% of the remainder – especially those who did not leave the Caribbean until after the age of 8 – had fairly vivid memories of childhood

75. Person(s) responsible for child's upbringing

60% said their mother
30% said parents, or mother and father
10% included grandmother and/or foster-parent

76. Place of birth

81% were born in Britain
19% were born in the Caribbean

77. Age of coming to Britain (if born in the Caribbean)

Wide-ranging

78. Parents' memories of transition

Less than 1% of parents had shared their experience of transitional difficulties or other related memories with their children

79. Earliest awareness of race or difference

10% gained such awareness at primary school
30% early in secondary school
50% (approximately) between ages 13–16
The remaining 10% still have no awareness of race or difference

80. Earliest realisation of parents' culture

65% said through food
25% said through speech

81. Awareness of other differences

25% were aware that their parents' child-rearing practices differed from the norm in this country

82. Awareness of language difference

10% had inferred a language difference from their inability to talk to teachers at the teachers' level

In the main, speech differences were recognised but not seen in terms of language difference

83. Awareness of Westindian culture

95% said they were aware of the existence of a Westindian culture, but could define few of its characteristics
90% regarded themselves as part of that culture

84. Reasons for feeling part of Westindian culture

Virtually all said this was because of their parents and their colour

85. Black British or just Black

Of those born in Britain
55% saw themselves as Black British, and
31% as just Black.
14% said Westindian rather than Black British or just Black

86. Westindian or African

All saw themselves as Westindian rather than African

87. Identification

All identified with Westindians, citing relatives and other connections as their reasons (food and life-styles also mentioned)

88. Family link with a specific island

90% identified themselves with their parents' island of origin

89. Choice between parents' and friends' life-styles

92% said they would choose that of their parents if a choice were necessary, the reason being that they preferred their parents' life-style to that outside of it

90. Attitude towards the extended family

84% said they liked the extended family network, although
95% had to have the meaning explained to them

91. Support from extended family

77% felt that they had the nuclear family here, but wished they could keep more in touch with other relatives both in Britain and in the Caribbean

92. British people's attitudes towards them

69% thought that British people did not like them
22% thought only *some* British people did not like them

93. Their attitude towards British people

95% felt negative towards the indigenous population
3% said 'I don't mind them,' 'They are OK sometimes,' or 'I like them, but . . .'
2% expressed positive feelings about British people

94. Attitude towards parents as compared with other people

98% said their attitude to their parents differed from their attitudes to other people
21% bracketed other relatives with their parents

95. Reason for difference in attitude

80% ascribed this difference to the respect they felt for their parents or to simple family feeling
Less than 5% cited anything to do with their parents' attitudes as a reason

96. Attitude towards British institutions in general

80% felt they were not fairly treated by British institutions
There was a general mistrust, implicit in statements such as 'They don't want to help us – they say they do, but they don't'

97. Specific British institutions

Over 90% of the above singled out the police as a prime example of the unfair treatment meted out to them
Less than 10% thought the police were fair
Less than 1% separated the police from the courts
About 50% said that schools treated them unfairly, but less than 10% singled out any other institution for such criticism

98. How British society sees them

62% thought they were not wanted here
72% thought they were regarded as second-class citizens
75% thought they were seen as being good at sport
Less than 1% felt British society saw them in a good light

99. Job expectations

Less than 10% had any clear expectations; the general feeling was that they would take whatever came along

60% wanted to work in an office

30% wanted to acquire engineering skills

100. Career ambitions

Over 50% had no idea how to go about fulfilling the ambitions they had

77% of those at school were very ambitious and would like to become professionals in skilled jobs

48% of those in work had lost ambition since starting

58% of school-leavers without jobs had abandoned all expectations or ambitions

101. Informal advice regarding career prospects

57% had no-one among family or friends to whom they felt they could turn for help or advice on careers

29% would only seek such help or advice from a relative or friend whom they saw as successful or doing well

Parents and friends were often said to be not in a position to advise or help, although a double-check revealed that many could in fact have done so but had not been asked

102. Family help in attaining career goals

81% felt that their family could not help them in attaining their career goals

10% felt the family could help a little

87% did not know any specific way in which their family could help

103. Assessment of employability

95% thought education was the criterion of employability

104. Knowledge of the Manpower Services Commission

97% of those still at school knew nothing about the MSC or what it had to offer for young people

17% of school-leavers had heard about MSC

105. Relevance of MSC to job prospects

The tiny minority who had heard of MSC thought it did some good, but did not really know

SCHOOL-LEAVERS ONLY (i.e. those who had left school)

106. Registering with careers office or jobcentre on leaving school

78% of school-leavers had registered with the local careers office
22% had registered immediately with a jobcentre

107. Reason for not registering or ceasing to register

84% of school-leavers had either failed to register or had taken their names off the careers office register, considering it a waste of time

108. Use of careers offices

Careers offices were seldom visited by those registered there

109. Attitude towards careers offices

They were generally thought to be unhelpful to Black people, though no clear reasons were given for such a conclusion; vague allusions were made to false expectations and slowness in responding

110. How, where and with whom jobless school-leavers spent their time

The picture was vague and unstructured, but hanging around with friends and going to clubs appeared to be the fashion except in those who were churchgoers
Less than 5% did anything structured
97% regarded the company of friends as important

111. Attitude of jobless towards employment

56% of unemployed school-leavers said they wanted to pick and choose despite their lack of skills and/or training
33% said they would do any work for the money

112. Attitude of jobless towards parents' employment

55% did not want to do the same job as their parents and felt that the latter only did them because they could not do anything else

113. Attitude to supplementary benefit

62% believed being on supplementary benefit was degrading and would rather work than receive it
34% felt they were entitled to it

EMPLOYED SCHOOL-LEAVERS ONLY

114. First job after leaving school

Those who had jobs had taken between two months and a year to find work after leaving school

71% did not hold their first job for longer than 3 months

115. Information about jobs

38% got their information about jobs from parents and friends
20% got this information from jobcentres

116. MSC job training/experience

Less than 1% had had any job training under an MSC scheme

117. Leisure time

71% wanted to pursue (or were already pursuing) leisure activities in which music played an important part – e.g., discos, dancing, clubs, church choirs

Members of Black-led churches spent most of their leisure time in church activities, formal or informal

Less than 1% went to the theatre
Less than 12% went to the cinema
Less than 1% went to professional football or cricket matches
Less than 2% attended any organised sporting occasions

118. Attitude to work

Almost all thought their work was good but too routine

119. Length of working week

Answers indicate those involved had little sense of time

120. Shift work

Less than 1% did shift work

ALL INTERVIEWEES

121. Plans for future training

85% of those still at school expressed a desire to be trained in a chosen field

87% of school-leavers had plans for future training

122. Plans for further education

68% of those at school planned to go on to further education
90% of school-leavers had no such plans

123. Attitude to Department of Employment

97% of those at school thought a Department of Employment was a good thing. However –
Less than 50% of school-leavers thought so

124. Peer group influence on choice of employment

71% said the peer group had no such influence
However –
31% admitted that they were discouraged or cried down by their peers if they went after something regarded as prestigious

125. Peer group influence on choice of life-style

88% said the peer group had no influence on their choice of life-style, although a strong but unacknowledged influence was very much in evidence

126. Peer group influence on attitudes to other people

74% said that the peer group had no influence on their attitude towards the family or friends or others
25% said that they experienced this influence only in respect of their attitudes to new friends
In general the influence of the peer group on attitudes was unacknowledged

127. Attitude towards Asians

97% said they had no dealings or did not mix with Asians
31% said they had met Asians at school
3% said they had friends among them

128. Attitude towards Jews and other ethnic groups

78% had no particular attitude, having given no thought to it

129. Attitude towards other Blacks

No attitude was expressed directly, but it emerged that
62% did not think well of other Blacks

130. Problems due to colour

73% thought they had problems because of their colour

131. Problems in the future

90% thought they would experience problems in the future because of their colour

132. Similar problems among relatives

60% thought their relatives had the same problems as themselves

133. Similar problems among other Blacks

84% thought other Blacks had the same problems as themselves

134. Similar problems among their parents

80% thought their parents did *not* have the same problems

135. Similar problems among White people

15% thought that White people had the same problems

136. Overcoming of problems

90% did not foresee their problems being overcome
65% gave their colour as the reason

137. Class barrier/alienation

60% thought there was a class barrier and that Blacks were in a 'stay-where-you-are' situation

138. Class to which they belonged

40% thought middle-class
41% thought working-class
19% said 'bottom' or below working-class

139. Attitude towards parental discipline

20% objected to outside influence in conflict situations with their parents
72% accepted that parents had the right to administer discipline

140. Attitude towards scolding

80% thought their parents had the right to scold them

141. Attitude towards types of punishment and restraint

89% did not approve of physical force or threats to make them do what they did not wish to do
44% thought corporal punishment did not solve anything or make any difference
53% would prefer withdrawal of privileges to beating as a punishment

142. Attitude towards self-discipline

The majority thought they were self-disciplined, but admitted that they might sometimes be otherwise

143. Attitude to having a totally free hand

68% did not consider total freedom a good thing

144. Make-up of household

65% did not have their biological father living with them as part of the household
36% had a step-father
28% had step-brothers or -sisters

145. Knowledge of biological father

21% did not know their biological father

146. Knowledge of father's whereabouts

47% did not know where their father lived

147. Father's occupation

81% of fathers did unskilled jobs

148. Mother's occupation

84% of mothers did unskilled jobs

149. Parents' attitude to life in Britain

65% thought that their parents did not like it in Britain
34% said that their parents would like to emigrate to the USA or Canada
35% thought that their parents would like to return to the Caribbean

150. Parents' attitude towards fellow Westindians

60% of parents had a lot of Westindian friends
Less than 10% mixed with Westindians from their own island but not with those from other islands
35% of parents appeared to have cut off from Westindian friends without replacing them, preferring to stay at home and have no social life

151. White friends

41% had White friends at school
Less than 2% continued this friendship after school

152. Parents' White friends

81% had no White friends

153. Invitations into White homes

Less than 5% had been invited into a White home

154. Mixed sporting activities

70% participated in sports alongside White teenagers

155. Involvement with courts

39% had had some involvement with the courts (either themselves or their family)

156. Feelings about parental experiences generally

51% thought that their mother had a hard time bringing up her children on her own

157. Feelings about parental experiences in the Caribbean

75% said that their parents never discussed their experiences of life in the Caribbean with them

158. Feelings about parents' migration to Britain

62% thought their parents would be better off in the Caribbean
98% felt they did not have a choice as to whether to come here

159. Feelings about returning to the Caribbean

85% of those born in the Caribbean would like to return there, but –
Less than 15% of those born in Britain wished to do so

160. Attitude to religion

98% believed in God
25% regarded themselves as Christian rather than religious

161. Parental attitude to religion

35% felt their parents did not practise what they preached and therefore disliked their attitude to religion

162. Parental attitude to involvement with opposite sex

72% thought their parents would not mind them being involved with opposite sex, but
41% had no such involvement so did not really know

163. Attitude to curfews

Curfews were considered unrealistic by the over-16s, especially where 9 or 10 p.m. was the outer limit

164. Parental attitude to clothes and hairstyle

Most felt that there was nothing bad about their parents' attitude to the clothes and hairstyle they (the children) chose to wear

165. Parental attitude to smoking

80% of parents did not approve of their children smoking

166. Parental attitude to drinking

It was felt that parents did not mind their children drinking in moderation at parties, but would not like them going into pubs

167. Parental attitude to choice of friends

65% said their parents insisted that friends must be 'decent and respectable', but criteria for this were ill-defined

168. Parental criticism of friends

85% said their parents criticised them for the company they kept or made disparaging remarks about their friends

169. Entertaining friends at home

54% said their parents did not encourage them to bring friends home
68% said their parents did not discourage them from bringing friends home

80% thought their parents might allow them to bring home friends considered well-behaved or liked by the parents, but not other friends (no clear-cut criteria)
31% said they took advantage of a change in their parents' attitude

170. Disagreement with parents and siblings

There were many altercations, but it was difficult to assess the degree of disagreement with parents or with brothers and sisters. Strong undercurrents were far more evident than open differences

171. Attitude to disagreements

62% blamed their parents for lack of understanding
Almost all felt lack of understanding was mutual where their brothers or sisters were concerned

172. Attitude to marriage

97% thought marriage was a good thing and wanted to marry one day

175. Attitude to having a family

98% would like to have a family

174. Attitude to size of family

80% wanted to have two or three children

175. Best age to marry and start a family

81% thought in their early 20s was the best age to marry and start a family

176. Home responsibilities

94% said their parents expected them to help with the housework
80% said they helped with the housework

177. Younger siblings' home responsibilities

80% said younger sisters were expected to help with the housework
65% said younger brothers were expected to do so

178. Desired age of leaving home

Most girls of school age said they would leave home when they got married, and most boys of school age said they wanted to do so between the ages of 19 and 22. School-leavers aged 17–19 had not yet left home

Review of Research Findings

i. Westindian teenagers at school

The feelings of Westindian teenagers towards school were very mixed. 41% did not go to school expecting to learn anything, but treated it as a place where they could meet with their friends, as home restrictions made it difficult for them to socialise outside of school. This answer emerged after studying a number of other answers under other profiles.

The attitudes of 92% towards school were determined by the attitudes of the teachers themselves. Attempts to communicate in a different register from that used in the children's homes result in slights and hurts which are not intended by teachers, but which are nevertheless very real to the children. Once a child believes that a teacher does not like him individually or because he is Black, hostility sets in and becomes very difficult to counteract. In the majority of cases this hostility was expressed in the playground among the peer group, rather than in the form of an open challenge to teachers.

84% said that they had a good relationship with one or more teachers, but only 26% said that they enjoyed a good teacher/pupil relationship with staff as a whole. Only 6% admitted not being able to communicate with teachers, yet it emerged that as many as 79% had some difficulty in comprehending what a teacher was saying. At no time was this deficiency in communication put down to language difficulties. Many children were getting into trouble for talking and not paying attention, when in fact all they were doing was asking their neighbour or friend to tell them what the teacher had said. 56% felt that asking a teacher to repeat things they did not understand would be seen as inattentiveness. Almost half the children were deterred from asking questions for this reason.

One obvious implication of these research findings is that the variety of English spoken by Westindian children needs to be treated virtually as a foreign language, and that if such an approach were to materialise their performance at school could well improve considerably. Language was undoubtedly a factor in their underachievement; more than 50% – the majority of them born in Britain – did not place the same conceptual meaning on many everyday expressions and experiences as would a member of the indigenous population. Moreover, teachers were unaware of this. Clearly teachers and children are operating in different linguistic registers, although both believe they have a common language and conceptual system.

Westindian children, like other children, relate to school in an emotional way and respond to teachers at an emotional level. But because teachers are unprepared by their training to deal with the emotional needs of Westindian children in particular, their responses often lead to poor performance. Of the 79% who did not always understand teachers, few gave reasons that could be considered valid or even rational. Failure to understand a teacher was put down to a dislike for the teacher or the teacher's dislike for them. Another highly emotive area is criticism; whether from parents or teachers, it appears to fuel alienation rather than lead to the desired improvement in performance or attitude. The majority of those interviewed had distanced themselves from their unpleasant experiences at school, and in many cases this had also developed into alienation both in the home and with regard to society as a whole.

Severe alienation at the time of leaving school can effectively reduce children who may once have been bright and insouciant to the level of emotional cripples. Such young people are unable to cope with the requirements of the labour market. Boredom, inability to get up in the mornings, bad attitudes to work and/or employers, lack of discipline – these are some of the symptoms of a deep disturbance rendering these young people unemployable until the condition is treated. Ironically, Westindians see schools as a training ground for attaining social mobility through the acquisition of academic and professional qualifications. Yet they would seem to be unaware that material achievement by their children in those areas has much to do with the assistance offered by the home. Parents without a tradition of study themselves appear unable to create a learning climate for their children.

The majority of those interviewed found teachers and school strange, but few admitted it. The same child who would say that he did not find school strange would go on to say that school was completely different in every way to home, and only 18% defined strange as differing from the usual or ordinary. Over 70% defined it as odd or peculiar, clearly indicating that they were conceptualising in Westindian terms although most of them were born in Britain.

32% of those at school said they would like help with English. 95% said they liked reading, yet less than 10% did any serious reading, comics being the most popular form of reading. Comprehension of the written word was a problem for 25%, compared with the 22% who had serious difficulty comprehending teachers. None of those interviewed had learnt anything at school about their parents' background. Less than 5% had learnt anything at all about the West Indies there, and what little they did learn had not helped them in any way with their identification problem. Less than 1% had learnt anything about slavery, and 98% did not associate it with their own history. None knew the date slavery was abolished, including those who had done some history at school.

70% said they did well at school, but quite a number really meant that they got on well with their friends at school. 67% were part of a group at school. 95% thought they were popular with friends and 33% gave the impression that they would do anything to live out this popularity, real or imaginary, both in and out of school. Groups appeared to provide some form of cultural protection, frequently developing their own forms of language patterns. It would appear that Jamaican dialect is much the strongest, even among those whose parents originate from other Caribbean islands. It was felt that teachers seldom saw them as a group or related to them as a group, but that those who did so saw them as trouble-makers.

There seemed to be no structural pattern to the way groups operated or spent their time. 'Play' was the main reason given for the existence of a group, but just how much play actually goes on must be open to question. Groupings seem to be spontaneous occurrences, rather than being the result of any conscious decision or plan of the group. There was no cohesion or organisation among any grouping. Children clan together and draw on the group, but none give anything constructive to it or manifest any solidarity with other members of the group. 62% were not members of any youth clubs, but 30% had some attachment to local church groups, which they did not see as youth clubs. The word 'club' evidently had un-Christian and improper connotations to it. Less than 10% were members of any ILEA youth clubs.

The influence exerted by the peer group was obviously very strong, but individual members of the group seemed strangely reluctant to acknowledge this. Members of the peer group came under severe attack from parents, who tended to blame them for their child's every misdemeanour. 85% of parents criticised their children's friends for their dress, class, parental background, education, etc., even though in many cases this amounted to flagrant hypocrisy. They also demanded 'good behaviour' without making any attempt to define what in their eyes constituted good behaviour.

Groupings appear, therefore, to be unconsciously formed by children to protect themselves from attacks by parents and teachers, but far from helping them it simply means that a massive amount of identity problems remain unresolved. As a result, many Westindian children grow up refusing to have any dialogue with their parents or with society, and their chances of receiving help gradually recede to almost nil.

ii. Westindian school-leavers

The situation of Westindian school-leavers in relation to finding work is a dismal one. The transition from school to the world of work, like that from home to school at the age of five, is one that cannot be made by most Westindians in Britain without some form of assistance. But it appears that no real effort is being made to help the Westindian child make either of these crucial transitions. Careers offices, the existing agencies through which school-leavers are given such help, are inadequate for the needs of Westindians. The alienation begun at school makes it almost impossible for careers offices in their present form to cater for the needs of Westindian teenagers. To do so means abandoning institutionalised and ethnocentric ways of working, which are based on the assumption that methods developed to meet the needs of indigenous school-leavers are suitable for those from other ethnic groups.

The system of linking job-seeking youths to registered vacancies is not working. In fact, it is doubtful whether careers offices would be more successful even if there were many more jobs available for each Westindian school-leaver to choose from. The system fails to take into account the lack of achievement at school and the level of alienation brought by Westindian school-leavers to the world of work. Many of them are suffering from the kind of stress that leaves an individual mentally unready for the world of work. Furthermore, any difficulties careers offices may have in finding an immediate job placement for a young Westindian may be interpreted by the latter as prejudice, or as a form of subtle rejection. Delays due to the observation of standard bureaucratic procedures reinforce the ever-present distrust of the system, and an unfruitful first attempt at securing a job for an individual may deter him from ever using a careers office again.

Westindian parents are seldom in a position to help their children find work. Hardly any are employers themselves or know employers well enough to be of assistance. The few that try to help or consider that they could do so if asked, may not actually be of much use, since such advice as they are able to offer cannot always be said to come from the most informed sources.

Quite a number of Westindians of school-leaving age seem to be under pressure from parents to leave school. It would appear that the harsh economic realities faced by parents force them to put their children on the labour market in order to supplement the family income. Parents of those interviewed seemed unaware of the difficulties faced by school-leavers in finding employment. Failure to find work readily, whether because the youngster is ill-equipped for work or because jobs are scarce, can mean intolerable pressures being brought to bear on individuals either to find any work they can get, no matter what the conditions, or at least to lay their hands on some money. Such pressure was usually greater among two-parent families than ones with a single parent, who generally offered more encouragement to stay on at school. It was evidently not unusual for school-leavers to give all their supplementary benefit to hard-pressed parents.

This research bears out the fact that many Westindian teenagers leave school and enter the world of work or unemployment already burdened by unbearable problems and pressures. Small wonder that many either resign themselves to drudgery or simply give up. All in all, the picture is depressingly bleak and does not look like being changed in the near future.

iii. Overall Conclusions

Westindian youth stands alone and isolated. They are given no positive help in learning to respect themselves. They are given no encouragement in developing as a group, and such individualism as this generates is not likely to be characterised by autonomy and initiative. Individualism and organisation are incompatible, because organisation demands that the needs of the individual be submerged to those of the group. The foundation is not there for active cooperation and the coming together of Westindian youth in an organised manner. The recent riots and those that preceded them in the early 1980s were nothing more than instantaneous flare-ups, symptoms of a more deeply-rooted problem which barely surfaced in itself. There is no basis for any highly-organised response to the many grievances Westindians have as a group. But far worse than these brief disturbances will undoubtedly happen if something is not done *now*, before it is too late – and the classroom is the best place to start.

The crucial questions of language, racism, stress and attitudes are dealt with subsequently in separate sections, but the principal issues of the research investigation may be summarised as follows:

WHY ARE WESTINDIAN TEENAGERS UNDERACHIEVING AT SCHOOL AND AT WORK?

A major causal factor is stress: the stress of living in a society that devalues them because of their skin colour. Among the debilitating symptoms of this condition are a lack of confidence and self-esteem, poor sense of aspiration, low breaking-point and an inability to cope with the challenges and demands of their situation in Britain. Beyond stress the most important factor is language interference. The assumption that British teachers and Westindian children have a common conceptual system because they both speak English is both erroneous and damaging. This investigation seems to bear out the fact that the variety of English spoken by most children of Westindian origin differs significantly from Standard English.

WHAT LIES BEHIND THEIR INDIFFERENCE TO SOCIETY AND THEIR PARENTS?

It would appear that they are not indifferent at all, either to society or to their parents. On the contrary, they are over-sensitive and highly vulnerable. They are emotionally aware of everything around them and tend to internalise every slight, real or imaginary. The apparent air of indifference surrounding them is only a defence mechanism, a shield to hide behind and, in many cases, has progressed to a form of chronic mental disturbance. It is almost certainly induced by living under prolonged stress from an early age, and affects Westindian teenagers in many different ways and with varying degrees of severity. Part of the result is a rejection of the parental work ethic, with many children refusing even to consider jobs – even if available (such as factory or transport work) – that their parents are willing to do but which their offspring see as stigmatised.

WHAT DETERMINES THEIR ATTITUDES, RESPONSES AND LIFE-STYLES?

British society as a whole must bear the main responsibility for what is happening to Westindians in this country. There is almost a kind of war between British society and Westindian youth, for many of whom life in Britain has either become intolerable or is just one great big 'dare'. Putting it at its simplest, Westindians in Britain are disadvantaged because this society is not Westindian and fails to acknowledge or provide for any Westindian cultural peculiarities. To make matters worse, the extent of that disadvantage is barely recognised even among Westindians themselves.

The disadvantaged face a tremendous uphill task if they are to reach the level of non-disadvantage – this before they can even begin to think of positive advantage. There is no short cut, as many appear to believe, often with tragic consequences. Westindian youngsters frequently exacerbate their problems and deepen their disadvantage by swimming across or against the tide, not realising that this is their downfall and that their difficulties in reaching the mainstream only increase.

On the other hand, society itself is engaged in the equally dangerous game of doing nothing and assuming that the current will carry these youngsters along and enable them eventually to join up with the mainstream. But if a person cannot swim, through no fault of his own, and either has a defective lifeline or no lifeline at all thrown to him, he is certain to drown. If the results of this investigation are anything to go by, that is precisely what is happening to Westindian youth.

PART 4

POSTSCRIPT

Language and Communication Problems

i. The Psychology of Language

Language may be said to be the expression of thought or thoughts which are conceived in the mind. Anyone attempting to analyse how language develops must therefore understand the process of conception. And, in order to understand this process, it is necessary to understand another process, that of *per*ception. This is the basic psychology behind the development of that articulate and generally coherent form of communication which we call language.

Perception is a form of cognition whereby things outside us are apprehended or grasped by the mind, i.e., the mental process of being aware of an external thing. The nerve-endings in our sensory organs are stimulated and this gives rise to a sensation – of sight, for example. Up to this point it seems to be a purely physical process. But our mental recognition of the fact that the sensation is coming from outside, the hallmark of *homo sapiens*, means that the sensation takes on an added significance when linked to our experience. We see a form which our eyes present to us as a rectangular-shaped object with certain markings on it; human intelligence instantly links this to the established concept of a book.

Perception is, therefore, concerned with particular objects and our discernment of them. *Con*ception, however, is the apprehending of particular things in a much more general sense. A concept may be defined as a general idea of similar things that is derived from familiarity with particular instances. We may have a concept of something concrete, such as a shop or a hospital, or of an abstract quality, such as squareness or roundness. Our experience tells us that there are many different breeds of horses, but the concept 'horse' represents the general idea – i.e., not of any one particular horse. Minor differences notwithstanding, any animal with attributes that fit our concept of a horse will be placed in that category.

Whether the object concerned is a horse or a house or a boat, it is clear that a process of abstraction is involved in the formation of concepts. This becomes apparent especially when we try to describe something to another person, for the very act of utilising the various tools of communication available to us is one of the ways in which we organise our experiences into abstractions. But this does not necessarily make us into abstract thinkers. The process is undoubtedly a mental act, but the awareness of this mental act should not be confused with that which is apprehended.

Without perception, therefore, you cannot have conception, just as you cannot have perception without sensation. When we perceive an object we name it, and this we are often enabled to do by our experience of objects sharing a common element or basically similar attributes that link them together. It is here that language comes in. First we form concepts, then we name these concepts by means of language. This makes language not merely a helpful tool of communication, but an indispensable aid to thought itself.

Language may be simply defined as a system of signs or names for identifying concepts or universals. If 'A' wishes to communicate something to 'B', he can do this, up to a point, through language consisting of natural, imitative signs. Beyond this he will generally find the use of words, spoken or written, to be the most efficient means. If 'A' and 'B' are from entirely different societies, they will obviously be dependent on the most rudimentary sign language – the classic 'Tarzan and Jane' situation. They will almost certainly have far less difficulty understanding one another if they belong to the same society but are both deaf and dumb (and have been so from birth). In this case, 'A' and 'B' will similarly resort to visible sign language, but within a particular society it is likely that a generally agreed system or pattern of signs and symbols will have emerged and become established.

The great disadvantage of relying on gestures or sign language for communication is that it takes a mime artist of rare genius to be able to represent silently the more intricate concepts and experiences which speech is capable of conveying with relative ease. To the deaf mute this renders inaccessible a rational understanding or interpretation of many complex phenomena taken for granted by most human beings. But even those with all their faculties intact, and who ostensibly speak the language of the person talking to them, may find themselves facing difficulties not unlike those of a deaf mute. 'A' and 'B' may be able to communicate in ordinary language, but 'A' must ensure that there is in 'B''s mind a conceptual scheme consistent with his own; if not, 'B' must be helped to develop this if he is to grasp fully what 'A' is talking about.

Few people appear to be aware that what may be termed the European conceptual system is lacking in the great majority of Westindian children, some of whom have, in effect, become deaf mutes as a result.

ii. The Language of Westindians

The clear implication of the foregoing remarks is that in order for people to communicate effectively, they must share a common conceptual system, which is the basis of a good rapport. It is my contention that no common conceptual system, and therefore no rapport, exists between Westindian children and their teachers in British schools. The tragedy of the whole situation is that neither teacher nor child is aware of this; both are assuming that they have a common conceptual system. In fact, the variety of English spoken by Westindians, though it contains many words in common with Standard English, might as well be a sign language for all its communication value in a British school as things stand.

English as spoken in the Caribbean is a patois generally called 'Creole', like its French and Dutch equivalents. But, in fact, almost all English-speaking Westindians speak a mixture of Creole and Standard English that is really neither one thing nor the other. In Britain this places them in a kind of linguistic no-man's-land which is symbolic of their situation in an overall sense. Even this 'mesolect' contains sufficient discrepancies in vocabulary and concept formation to make it a language on its own, as foreign to English as French and Dutch Creole are to the languages of France and Holland respectively. But whereas the authorities in those two countries have long recognised these differences and have acted accordingly, Britain has continued to ignore the implications, despite their obvious relevance to the poor performance of Westindian children in British schools.

Many of these children say that they have no trouble understanding the teacher, without realising that they are making a false assertion. The reality is that when they first set foot in a classroom at five years old, they only partially understand their teachers and this sets in motion a pattern which continues right the way through their early school careers and beyond, because they take it as the norm and no-one disabuses them. One result of this is that many grow up with the erroneous impression that competition is not important in this world. Some reach a stage where they think it is only necessary to hear the words, without bothering to grasp the real meaning. Others are conscientious and alert, but mistake their attentive listening for understanding.

Very few Westindian children are aware of the power of language as a tool of communication. They fail to see this because they lack the reasoning skills which most of us take for granted: the ability to rationalise in a language, to build up an argument, and so on. They either genuinely believe they are understanding the teacher, or get into the habit of saying that they have understood without really understanding at all – and you cannot realistically expect someone with a deep feeling of insecurity to admit that they have failed to grasp something. A good teacher will not ask such individuals directly 'Have you understood?', but will encourage the class generally to speak up with impunity ('Would anyone like to give me their version of what I've said?'), so that understanding becomes a serious thing. Unfortunately, the more insecure an individual pupil, the more likely he is to treat it all as a big joke.

If someone is speaking to you about something, you have to be drawing a kind of picture in your mind, illustrating whatever it is that is being said. That is what is really meant by understanding language. It is not just knowing, for example, that Kingston is in Jamaica; if someone is talking about Kingston, Jamaica, it is a question of understanding the nuances and descriptions and everything else, so that if asked to write an essay about it, you could put it in your own words because you have fully understood. That is comprehension, and anyone having difficulty with comprehension, either in terms of the written word or of the spoken word, has a communication problem.

An Englishman might be able to read and write fluently in French, but that does not mean that he will necessarily understand a Frenchman speaking to him. In other words, he does not have the mastery of French possessed by a native speaker – even one who cannot read or write particularly well. He therefore has a communication problem in that language, and this would be a considerable disadvantage to him if speaking and comprehending it were a vital part of his daily life. If someone was very sarcastic to him in French he would probably take him literally, and this might easily land him with all manner of problems.

Similarly, Westindians generally do not have a mastery of the English language. This has been demonstrably true for almost all the youngsters with whom we have dealt over the years. Had one said to them 'If you do so-and-so, I will do so-and-so,' nine out of ten would not have heard the 'if' at all. They would have turned up expecting to be given what they thought had been promised, even though they had failed to fulfil the condition which was part of the agreement. They would actually have felt cheated, although it was all down to a lack of comprehension on their part.

Language skills and reasoning may not be called for when you are talking about cricket or reggae. But they most certainly are needed in the world of ideas, especially ideas to do with learning, which is what teachers are generally trying to convey. The inability to register or pick up on these ideas is one of the main stumbling blocks for Westindian children. And when pupils are unable to retain for future use anything told them by the teacher, or seem unable to act upon it, the teacher's expectations of them are likely to be fairly low unless the nature of this problem of communication is recognised. All too often these low expectations in turn affect the child, becoming what has been aptly termed a 'self-fulfilling prophecy'.

The four statements given as part of Westindian Concern's evidence to the Rampton Committee of Inquiry (see pp. 37–39) all demonstrate the general lack of awareness among teachers and educationalists as to the nature of the problem. The fallacy that these youngsters were English-speaking led to inaccurate assessments of their capability. 'Poor communication skills', 'inability to learn', 'very slow learner' and ' trouble-maker' were some of the dismal classifications blandly applied to them, although their performance in this research project totally belied these labels.

In London and other large urban areas, remedial education for such children has long been universally accepted as inevitable. Boroughs with a high proportion of Westindian residents – such as Hackney, Haringey, Lambeth, Wandsworth and Brent – have traditionally assigned these children to schools for the educationally sub-normal. In 1975, Dr. Clifford Hill, Senior Lecturer at North East London Polytechnic, was able to produce a report showing that in all these boroughs Westindian children constituted an average 80% of the intake of ESN schools. The inclusion of Brent should have alerted the authorities to the possibility that a mistake was being made somewhere along the line. In an area where the Asian and Westindian communities were of similar size, why should Westindians still form 80% of those diagnosed as ESN? It may well be that the language difficulties of Asian children were recognised while those of Westindian children were not.

The suffering inflicted on children in this situation is an example of unintentional racism (see following section), which involves the assumption that everyone must be able to communicate in Standard English, with allowances being made only for those whose language is different in every way. Many teachers have unwittingly compounded the situation by referring to the variety of English spoken by Westindian children as 'bad English'. It is obviously very important for the language of Westindians to be recognised and used as the starting point, with Standard English being learnt as a second language, bearing in mind the comments in the preceding section about perception and conception in the crucial formative years. This would enable them at least to conceptualise in English as a foreign language.

This argument is vehemently rejected by those who preach assimilation rather than integration. But the simple and ironic truth is that the measures proposed here are only necessary because the parents and grandparents of these children received no help of any kind – least of all linguistically and conceptually – in adjusting from the Caribbean to the British way of life.

Racism in Britain

There is a common, but mistaken, assumption in this country that racists are all people with ill will towards Blacks. The phenomenon of racism extends, however, far beyond the frontiers of blind prejudice typified by organisations like the National Front; in fact, the worst offenders are often those with the very best of intentions. Such people do not call for the expulsion of Black people, nor do they proclaim openly that Whites are more intelligent, civilised, clean, cultured, etc. They merely assume these things, though often without realising it. They even bend over backwards to be helpful to ethnic minorities, but their fundamentally patronising approach betrays the underlying racist attitude with which the system has imbued them.

The most pernicious kind of racism, in a sense the father to all other kinds, is that which manifests itself (though seldom overtly) in systems of thought, language or society. In Britain we have, to our shame, a social and political system which has quietly and efficiently ensured that Black people have the most sub-standard housing, lowest wages, worst health provisions, poorest education, highest level of unemployment and severest police harassment – including an alarming rate of attacks on themselves and their property – of any group in this country. The evidence for all this is easily available but rarely publicised. It is what is known as institutional racism, which the Swann Report described aptly as 'the way in which a range of long established systems, practices and procedures, both within education and the wider society, which were originally conceived and devised to meet the needs and aspirations of a relatively homogeneous society, can now be seen not only to fail to take account of the multi-racial nature of Britain today but may also ignore or even actively work against the interests of ethnic minority communities.'[17]

Those of us who happen to be Black thus find ourselves surrounded by institutions which assume we are inferior without actually saying so. Everything they do is to 'civilise' us, to make us more like them, to work on us subtly and get us to conform, thereby making us acceptable or palatable to the people of this country. All this is done, not in a grudging or uncharitable spirit, but with a *missionary zeal*. They put a lot of love and care into it, and their pleasure is genuine when they see us achieving on merit. The fact that in order to do this we have to divest ourselves of everything that made us what we are, and become Europeanized in all but skin, is conveniently ignored. Such precepts and assumptions are taken for granted by the majority, and many would regard them as the best gift one could possibly bestow on others. The harm done in this way is mostly unwitting, because racist practice among the British commonly masquerades as a national pride in their way of doing things. Sadly, the heirs to the collective genius which pioneered the Industrial Revolution fail to recognise that many other nations have now surpassed them.

In 1984 the Policy Study Institute published its third report on racial discrimination and disadvantage. The evidence showed that little had improved since its report of 10 years earlier, and that some things had even got worse. People in Britain talk about a multi-racial society, but few appreciate that it must also be a multi-cultural society; and it cannot be a multi-cultural or, indeed, a just and balanced society if just one ethnic group – albeit the strongest, indigenous one – dictates all the terms and makes all the rules as to what constitutes proper conduct, with 'good' professional work practice always being determined in an ethnocentric manner grounded in British and European traditions. British society has signally failed to make the necessary adjustments to accommodate other racial groups, preferring to bludgeon them into conformity if they wish to make this country their home.

For the Westindian child at school in Britain, there is little chance of escaping the effects of this, not only because the education system itself is one of the pillars of institutional racism, but because the whole climate in which the child is growing up is permanently infected with a racist bias. Even the Rampton Interim Report admits that 'there is considerable evidence that discrimination, both intentional and unintentional, can have an adverse effect on how a West Indian child sees himself and his ethnic group in relation to majority white society which can in turn have a bearing on his motivation and achievement.'[18] But, unfortunately, neither Rampton nor Swann offers anything like a remedy for this state of affairs.

An important element in this is the fact that there is no such thing as neutral education in this country. Because of this, many Westindians have been educated into supporting racism, and thus give the lie to the spurious notion that you cannot be a racist if you are Black. Racism is a self-perpetuating phenomenon because the only people – White or Black – who are listened to by the system, are those who have been trained within it and have not rebelled. Such people obviously have nothing controversial to say.

We ourselves know of a Westindian who was educated at Cambridge. His wife is English and they are still devoted to one another after many years of marriage, during which time they have had several children. He is quite prepared to admit that he is a racist. After graduating he felt it necessary to go for elocution lessons, knowing that he was unlikely to succeed with a Jamaican accent. They have striven to ensure that their children have identical life-styles to their neighbours, in the hope that their children would not feel at a disadvantage. They never eat Westindian food, and if one visits them one cannot drop in unannounced, as is the norm among Westindians. Visitors have to give notice of their intention even to make a casual call.

It is clear that the English wife/mother has, perhaps understandably, tried to establish a normal English household to the exclusion of all things Westindian. The children are unable to relate to their Westindian peer group and go all out to imitate their White friends. This places them under considerable stress and strain when they find they are not accepted as equals by society.

No doubt the husband is the model anglicised Black man from an establishment point of view, and good luck to him; but the Westindian community as a whole is never going to make advances in this country while its own people continue to feel such a denial of their origins is necessary and desirable.

The Stress Factor

The relationship between stress and underachievement among Westindians in Britain is one which had begun to dawn on us long before the research programme got underway, but the full significance and substantiality of that relationship registered only when we listened afterwards to over 600 hours' worth of interviews on tape. The horrifying truth came over all too clearly, as one interviewee after another spoke of his or her attitudes and experiences, often with a nonchalance or dispassion that betrayed an ill-concealed undercurrent of gloom, discomfort and bewilderment.

A documentary film made in the USA had already given us some intimation of the impact of psychological disadvantage on children's performance at school. Called *The Eye of the Storm*, the film concerned an experiment carried out as part of a large research programme into the effects of prejudice. In cooperation with parents and the authorities, a teacher had introduced to her class the idea that blue-eyed children were superior to those with brown eyes. Very soon the performance of those pupils with blue eyes began to show a dramatic improvement, while the brown-eyed children fared considerably worse than they had done before and manifested signs of stress and unhappiness with attendant behavioural problems. Happily, this was only a demonstration and all ended well, but the implications are clear enough.

Stress, however, is one of the most commonly misunderstood and misinterpreted phenomena in Western society. It can take any number of forms, of which a clinically treatable mental disorder is only one example – and a much rarer one than is generally supposed or realised. Because of the extraordinary amount of misunderstanding and mystification that surrounds the concept of stress – particularly among Westindians, to whom it represents something fearful and ungodly – we quote below an article which appeared some years ago in the American scientific journal *Psychology Today*. In it, the world's leading stress researcher, psychologist Hans Selye, answers questions about stress in relation to his own life. It was he who, half a century ago, borrowed the term 'stress' from physics to describe the body's responses to everything from common ailments to emotions such as fear and anger. His remarks, especially those concerning what he calls 'purposelessness', are as lucid and as apt an explanation of the subject as one could hope to find.

Q: How do you cope with stress?
A: By being as busy as I possibly can. I put in at least a ten-hour day – attending conferences, writing papers, making speeches. And far from being wearied by this schedule, I find that I flourish on it.

Q: Doesn't that contradict the advice we hear about slowing down to avoid stress?
A: Unfortunately, there's a great deal of confusion about what stress actually is and how we should deal with it. Stress is the body's non-specific response to any demand placed on it, whether unpleasant or pleasant.

Sitting in a dentist's chair is stressful. But so is exchanging a passionate kiss with a lover – after all, your pulse speeds up, your breathing quickens, your heartbeat soars. Yet who in the world would forgo such a pleasurable pastime simply because of the stress?

Our aim shouldn't be to avoid stress completely, which would be impossible, but to recognize our typical response to stress and then to modulate our lives accordingly.

We've discovered that there are two main types of human beings: 'racehorses', who thrive on stress and are happy only with a vigorous, fast-paced life-style, and 'tortoises', who need peace, quiet and a generally tranquil environment – something that would frustrate most racehorse types. I can hardly imagine any torture worse than having to lie on a beach day after day, yet a great many people aim to do precisely that.

We hear a great deal about the dangers of overwork and excessive striving, but I think this is exaggerated and arouses unnecessary anxiety. If a danger does exist, it is that some people mistake their own type and push beyond their normal stress endurance. That should be avoided.

Q: How can a person decide to which type he belongs?
A: By careful observation. Stress inventories in common use are flawed because they fail to give enough weight to individual differences. Each of us is the best judge of himself, and we can gradually develop an instinctive feeling that tells us whether we're running above or below the stress level that suits us best.

There are revealing body clues. Animals under stress show

increased body movement, as do humans. You may not be aware that you're under stress, but meanwhile you are gesticulating more and your heart rate has increased. There are also behavioural indicators, such as insomnia or irritability. Detecting stress isn't difficult once you're more self-aware.

Q: How valuable are drugs or relaxation techniques such as transcendental meditation in helping people cope with stress?
A: Rather than relying on drugs or other techniques, I think there's a better way to handle stress. Attitude determines whether we perceive any experience as pleasant or unpleasant, and adopting the right one can convert a negative stress into a positive one – something I call a 'eustress', employing the same Greek prefix for 'good' that occurs in such words as euphoria and euphony.

Q: Does positive stress, eustress, also place demands on the body?
A: Yes, but for reasons we can't yet explain far fewer demands. For example, I doubt if anyone could endure my busy schedule unless he took as favourable a view of the work as I do. For me it is not just an obligation but a pleasure. That makes it a eustress. Also, I've learnt through the years to forget unpleasant incidents. 'Imitate the sundial's ways, count only the pleasant days,' was a folk proverb I often heard growing up in Austria-Hungary, and it made a deep impression on me.

I find that I cannot bear grudges. If wronged by some friend or colleague, I may break off contact out of sheer self-protection, but I bear him little enmity. After all, nature gives even the most fortunate of us only a limited capital of energy to resist stress, and it would be silly to squander it on anger.

This same attitude helped me a few years ago when my doctor told me I had cancer and had only a few months to live. I refused to retreat from life and was determined to keep working without worrying about my end. Perhaps this attitude helped my body combat the stress of my disease and of subsequent operations, since, as you see, I am still ticking today.

Q: Do you think today's families or teachers fail to show us how to cope adequately with stress – possibly because the stresses themselves have increased?
A: Every era has been an age of anxiety. A few hundred years ago, for example, there was no threat of nuclear war, but there was the terrible danger of the plague, which quite literally

destroyed whole populations. And everything in human life is uncertain and contingent – you may be rich today and poor tomorrow, or healthy or sick; this has been true throughout history. However, there is one type of social stress that I think has particularly increased in our time: loss of motivation.

I first began to consider this problem in earnest when I noticed that my children and their friends seemed to be drifting, unsure of what to do with their lives – one of the most stressful situations imaginable. One of the most popular solutions offered as an answer to this dilemma appears to be the notion that you should live for yourself, without giving much thought to others.

Q: Isn't this attitude reflected in the host of best-sellers celebrating the virtues of selfishness and the wisdom of "looking after Number One"?

A: Yes, and up to a point that is wise. Human beings, like all organisms, are born egoists – they have to look out for themselves first. The fallacy is to confuse this natural phenomenon with egotism – the ruthless pursuit of your own ends. I doubt if there could be a more stressful approach to life, since it creates antagonism and enemies all around you.

Another fashionable antidote for loss of motivation, one embraced by many cults, requires absolute altruism and endless self-sacrifice. That approach, too, contains its own grain of truth. Just as we're all born egoists, so we're also born altruists. The danger is that altruism carried to an extreme violates our nature, the biological basis of life, and leads to stressful frustration and resentment.

As a scientist working in a laboratory, I learned that, on even the most primitive levels of life, there is a balance between altruism and egoism. Individual cells, at some point in the past, gave up their independence to form stronger and more complex beings. A cancer cell, by contrast, cares only for itself. It continues its reckless and egocentric development, feeding on its host until it kills it – and so commits suicide.

Going from the simplest level of life to the most complex, I noticed that most patients I've seen with stress-linked diseases also suffered from a warped code of behaviour – one that emphasized either too much selfishness or too much self-sacrifice.

Little by little, my own experience and scientific work have led me to develop a kind of recipe for the best antidote to the stresses of life. The first ingredient, as I told you, is to seek your own stress level, to decide whether you're a racehorse or a tortoise and to live accordingly. The second is to choose your goals and make sure they're really your own, not something imposed on you by others. And the third ingredient in this recipe is altruistic egoism – looking out for yourself by being necessary to others.

Q: But how many of us can be really necessary to those around us?
A: I think all of us can. You needn't discuss the equivalent of the theory of relativity or write the world's greatest symphony to achieve that state. You can work at being a good teacher, a good baker, a good neighbour. And striving to make yourself ever more useful and necessary is an aim you can safely pursue throughout your life, and one that will protect you from the worst of all modern social stresses, purposelessness.

It gives me pleasure to know that my stress research will outlive me. If it can teach others to be as happy and content as I am, by mastering the different stresses of life, I'll be satisfied indeed.'*

The experience of Westindian children in British schools has created a new breed of person that is neither fish nor fowl. On the one hand they have, in a sense, joined with the wider society in devaluing what their parents have to offer culturally, but on the other hand they have not been given the assistance or the skills they need to be part of the mainstream. Apart from the few who have managed to break free, they are a group of floundering individuals, in conflict both with their parents and with society as a whole. They have their own language which no-one but their peer group can understand, but far from creating a bond within the group this only furthers their isolation.

In a society that devalues Black people, coping with being Black is a formidable task in itself. Black British children of Westindian origin are even more vulnerable, since the destruction of the culture that is part of their heritage has left

* Reprinted and condensed with permission from *Psychology Today* Magazine © 1978 (APA).

them without much-needed support. They have become a prey to *acculturation* or creeping assimilation into a European value system in which they have no traditional grounding, and which is in conflict with the value system operating in Westindian homes.

The conflict experienced by Westindian youth, recognised or unacknowledged, has given rise to a high degree of stress which manifests itself in low self-esteem, poor motivation, depression and – in some cases, but not as many as the press and others appear to believe – an unacceptable level of anti-social behaviour. Any response to these manifestations that does not take in the stress factor is likely to be counter-productive because it will only increase a young person's resentment without doing anything at all to change things for the better.

Attitudes

i. The Nature of Attitudes

Attitudes relate to socialisation and individual social behaviour. An attitude may be said to be a psychological construct, since it cannot be observed directly by another person. The existence of an attitude can only be inferred from the introspective reports of the individual or from such elements as may be observed in his behaviour. An attitude should therefore be seen as a concept, rather than as a concrete reality, and as a something subjectively assessed and imputed to a person by others.

Various definitions have been proposed in the many writings on the subject. The following seem pertinent to the nature of this research:

> An attitude is a mental and neural state of readiness, organised through experience, exerting a directive or dynamic influence upon the individual's response to all objects and situations with which it is related.[19]

> An attitude is a mental disposition of the human individual to act for or against a definite object.[20]

> [Attitudes are] certain regularities of an individual's feelings, thoughts and predispositions toward some aspect of his environment.[21]

It seems, therefore, that a plausible theory of the nature of attitudes is one which incorporates the cognitive, the affective, the motivational and the behavioural.

ii. Formation of Attitudes

Implicit in the notion of the individual acting or responding to an object (person/event/group) or the environment, is the assumption that attitudes are learnt. A number of writers have drawn a distinction between attitudes and the closely related concept of opinions, beliefs and values which do not have the same behavioural import. Since attitudes are formed or moulded, the context in which this occurs greatly influences the outcome. Here the observations of Sherif and Sherif are crucial:

> Socialisation of the human child consists in large degree of the individual's internalisation of the values, norms, roles, and way of life in his family and that part of society in which he lives.[22]

This points directly to the dilemma of the Westindian child growing up in the UK. Whose norms and values does he/she internalise? Does the child absorb only one set of norms? To what extent does one internalise certain facets of racism, while reacting against it? Some may not even recognise racism, let alone show any reaction against it. This is likely to be the case at an early age. Stressful conditions will be the almost inevitable result if this conflict or 'clash of cultures' is not sensitively handled or resolved. The situation is so complex that many Westindian parents are unable to provide their children with the support they need to prevent them getting into a state of chronic ambivalence or alienation.

The socialisation process is many-faceted, but there are two elements that should be highlighted because of the way they impinge on the development of attitudes in the individual. One is the fact that attitudes are component parts of the person; the other is that attitude formation involves concept formation. If we accept these two things it is clear that we have a situation that is fraught with potential disquiet and tension. Self-image is one of the many concepts which human beings develop. Their attitudes may, therefore, be merely the outward manifestation of greater internal forces. In the case of Westindian youngsters, their passive and negative attitudes may be symptomatic of an invisible inner turbulence.

Attitudes are generally formed over a sustained period and therefore learning of them, as with school subjects, is a gradual process – though this does not take into account the immediate and profound impact on the individual of sudden, jolting encounters. Fundamental to the processes that shape attitudes are the informational content and emotional intensity of the learning experience. Attitudes are not merely instant reactions, and so there is a degree of permanence in them, but being part of one's learned behaviour they are not entirely irremediable or irreversible.

Some of the experiences that shape attitudes may well be vicarious, i.e., drawing on the experience of parents, siblings or peers. The attitudes of Westindian youngsters to institutions, groups, work and professional practices, are likely to be formed in this way. So, on the one hand, they may get information from siblings or the peer group that induce them to develop a particular attitude towards, for example, the police or authority in general; and on the other hand the experience of their parents with regard to housing and employment is likely to bring about a gradual awareness in them of the workings of racism. Both sets of attitudes will be further fuelled by an abundant variety of impressions and information gathered from the media.

iii. Attitudes among Westindian Youth

Side by side with the language, racism and stress factors looked at in the preceding sections, the attitudes of Westindian teenagers represent the most striking feature to emerge from the research – both individual and, more especially, overall attitudes. A large proportion of the questions asked sought to address this aspect of the Westindian experience, and most interviewees voiced some form of attitude towards (1) themselves, (2) their parents, (3) school, (4) teachers, (5) discipline/authority, (6) institutions, (7) the police, (8) employment, (9) family, (10) sex, (11) marriage, (12) religion, (13) immigration, (14) peer group/friends, (15) others' view of them, (16) British society, (17) ethnic groups. In addition some answers were obtained regarding parents' attitudes as interpreted by the interviewees.

Because of the integral part they play in shaping the self-image and feelings of self worth (i.e., attitude towards self), nos. 2–17 will be discussed before consideration of no. 1 and the general outlook.

Attitudes towards parents are generally positive, especially as compared with attitude towards others, the main reason being the obvious one of family ties. The most significant element in this is the positive attitude of 80% towards parental discipline and scolding, and the general feeling that total freedom would be inappropriate, belying the grave misgivings common among teachers concerning the strict and conservative child-rearing practices of Westindian parents. Conversely, the majority of interviewees had negative feelings about their parents' occupations and circumstances in this country. Many had been brought up by their mother on her own, and felt she had had a hard time in this.

However much school may have failed them, the attitude of Westindian teenagers towards school remains generally good. 90% felt positive about staying on at school, while 50% regarded leaving at the minimum school-leaving age as distinctly undesirable. It is sadly ironic that children who value education so highly should achieve so little in British schools.

By contrast their attitudes towards teachers often show considerable negativity, particularly their assessment of how teachers view them. The vital significance of this is dealt with in the concluding remarks below. Authoritarian discipline administered by parents, especially the use of dire threats or physical force to make children do things, is viewed very negatively except where manifestly warranted; such discipline administered by parents is considered more acceptable provided it is not excessive.

Distrust of Britain's institutions is common, in particular the feeling that promises are not kept and that genuine willingness to help Blacks is hard to find. The police, directly linked with the courts in the eyes of many, come in for by far the greatest criticism of any institution. Over 90% of those interviewed thought the police treated them unfairly – an overwhelming indictment of policing methods in areas with a high percentage of Westindian residents. Beyond this, any agency whose main function is to safeguard the British public by protecting the White-oriented status quo is bound to be unpopular among Blacks.

Attitudes to work generally, also towards particular jobs and unemployment, have already been examined in the general review of the research findings. The overall picture here is one of high aspiration poorly catered for and, in many cases, stifled by insensitive treatment or denial of opportunity. Basically positive attitudes are swiftly transformed by grim experience into negative ones.

Answers to questions concerning the 'extended family' system and having a family oneself reveal that Westindian teenagers feel positive about their own cultural traditions with regard to the family, but that some aspects of English family life definitely impinge on this – especially the common desire to marry and have a 'normal' family (two or three children). This causes conflict which can escalate to acute cultural confusion, reinforced as it is by experience and resultant attitudes in other spheres.

Attitudes towards the opposite sex are clearly influenced by the above, but the research yielded no significant data on this. Religion was also barely touched upon, although it is interesting to note that teenagers are somewhat critical of their parents' attitude to religion, the reason given being an apparent failure to 'practise what they preach'. Many parents have experienced so many problems in coming to terms with life in Britain that they can seem self-righteous and hypocritical in demanding exemplary behaviour from their children, including observance of religious principles.

Attitudes concerning a return to the Caribbean appear influenced to a great extent by the place of birth. As many as 85% of those born in the Caribbean expressed the desire to go back to live there, while among the British-born only 15% shared this sentiment. However, 62% of all interviewees, including many British-born, felt negative about their parents' migration to Britain. 65% thought their parents did not like it in Britain and would return to the Caribbean or emigrate to Canada or the USA given the chance.

Peer group influence and choice of friends is another subject covered in the general review of the research findings, the prime factor being the unconscious formation of groups as mutual protection societies. The need for such bulwarks against the workings of institutional racism, in schools and elsewhere, is further evidence of the almost impossibly steep uphill battle faced by Black people in this society. This is underlined by the attitudes of those interviewed towards British society and by what they felt to be other people's attitudes towards them. Negativity towards the indigenous population was almost universal. 62% felt they were not wanted in this country, 69% that British people did not like them, and more still that they were looked upon and treated as second-class citizens. Hardly anyone thought that the British public saw them in a good light.

Friendships or dealings of any kind with other ethnic groups appear to be very limited, and consequently attitudes are either equivocal or non-existent among Westindian teenagers in this area. Attitudes towards other Blacks in general are equally ill-defined, but a high proportion of unexpressed negativity is nevertheless in evidence here.

iv. Conclusion

It is abundantly clear that Westindian teenagers, including the majority of those born here, do not see themselves as a part of what they regard or perceive as the British people. As this unpalatable truth is all too easily seized upon by extreme right-wing groups as a justification for their odious activities, a rider must be added to it. Obviously they had no choice as to where they were born, and therefore to dwell on the issue of whether they should 'go back whence they came' is futile and witless as well as being highly detrimental to race relations. The implications for British society remain very serious.

It is surely small wonder, in the light of this and of the various attitudes outlined above, that Westindian children's attitudes towards themselves become progressively more negative, and that this negativity becomes more deeply entrenched as they get older.

Language, as we have seen, is a problem which can be dealt with in an entirely practical fashion; it remains only for the problem itself to be recognized and acknowledged. Racism is clearly endemic and will be with us for a long time to come, but again a willingness to recognize and expose it will do much to temper its worst excesses. Even stress among children and teenagers, for all its ugly connotations, is a relatively simple issue in that it can be relieved by parents and other caring individuals. Attitudes, however, are the hardest thing of all to combat – if only because they are embedded in the very deepest part of the psyche, forming the invisible battle lines that transcend even racial considerations.

No amount of equal opportunity provisions will be of any avail unless something is done to instil better attitudes in young Westindians, enabling them to develop confidence and feelings of self-worth as well as the capacity for relating to others. Westindians of all ages would benefit from this, but it is in the classroom above all – the traditional place for fundamental learning – that such inculcation should occur.

Apart from parents it is teachers who exercise the most influence on children's attitudes, and obviously the teachers' own attitudes play a large part in this. In fact, Westindian parents tend by nature to leave almost every aspect of education, including social and life skills, to the school. The high percentage of negative feelings expressed by interviewees regarding their teachers' attitudes is therefore all the more worrying. We are not concerned here with attitudes to particular subjects, but with interpersonal relationships between teachers and children. If a child develops a poor self-image at school, it is an indictment of his teachers and their failure to eradicate unhealthy attitudes, in themselves as much as in the child.

Clearly there is no magic prescription for all the problems

that exist. A few practical solutions are suggested later in these pages (see Appendix B), but no individual can possibly hold all the answers. These lie, of course, with society as a whole – the ultimate arbiter of civilised attitude and action.

Appendix A

Caribbean House

Caribbean House is a group of converted terraced houses in Bridport Place, Shoreditch Park, in the London Borough of Hackney. For the past decade Caribbean House has been carrying out a number of action research initiatives with one main objective in mind; that of assisting Westindians to draw on their own Westindian experiences as a vehicle for learning and understanding more about the Westindian community in the United Kingdom; the work has also included an examination of the Westindian situation in order to identify areas of concern and needs among this group through a number of inter-related projects. These projects were designed to respond to immediate crisis situations in an attempt to develop preventative strategies which would, as a result, reduce the high level of intervention, on the part of outside agencies, into the family situation. Many of the problems in black child-care, particularly those pertaining to children at risk, are due to lack of effective parental supervision and guidance.

In 1975 Westindian Concern Limited (see below) embarked upon the setting up of an AfroCaribbean Childcare Project aimed at reconciliation between Westindian children and their parents.

The organisation established a children's hostel as part of its family-centred child-care initiative, the purpose of which was to offer short-stay accommodation for children in conflict with their parents. This approach proved highly effective since it provided a breathing space for our Caseworkers to effect a reconciliation through intensive Family Casework, support and counselling.

By 1978 Caribbean House was able to close the children's hostel because from among the many families whom the organisation had helped emerged an extended family network. This family network was to become the backbone of the support offered to beleaguered parents. It also provided an extended family fostering resource whose participants not only offered that essential breathing space, but also afforded a higher level of emotional support to the children whose needs had been so identified by Caribbean House staff.

Today this extended family support network service numbers over one hundred black families, and is widely used as a resource by many Social Services Departments who may be experiencing difficulties in finding black foster parents.

A number of succesful action research programmes have been implemented and developed over the past ten years. Chief among these are:

Caribbean House Family Centred Child-Care Services

This Family Centred Child-Care Agency departs from the more traditional Child-Care practices which tend to be child-centred. A basic component of this service is that it draws on the strengths of the extended Westindian family, not only in Britain but in the Caribbean itself. With workers and officers in both the Caribbean and the UK, the organisation was uniquely placed to involve whole families irrespective of boundaries.

Family Counselling, with its extensive Family Casework, Family Support and Education provisions, is a major need and a valuable resource to the London Borough of Hackney. This project, which has up to now concentrated on helping children and their families in Hackney, is now in the process of extending its services at a national level, and is in a state of readiness to respond to the needs of other inner city Boroughs.

Caribbean House Education Unit

This unit offers youth counselling, educational guidance, intermediate treatment, social and life skills to alienated black youth. It provides courses in parenting, educational assessments and psychological testings for children where appropriate.

Caribbean House Employment Agency

This project offers job and vocational training, work placements, work experience, career advice and the acquisition of job-seeking skills. The development of communication skills and skills to seek employment outside one's local region are also on offer.

Caribbean House Business Enterprises

There is an economic development aspect to Caribbean House

– the organisation is striving to develop a number of economic and employment creation initiatives in order to generate more of its own income for its Community Development Programme. Projects already operating are:

A Community Restaurant with outside catering facilities
A Community Food Shop with home delivery facilities
An Employment & Travel Agency for the elderly and the housebound
A Printing and Photographic Service
Building Contractors
Publishers and Booksellers

Anglo-Caribbean Social Work Agency
An international social service facility. Caribbean House is developing services in the Caribbean area for the Westindian elderly living in the U.K. Caribbean House Barbados opens in April 1986; Caribbean House Jamaica and Caribbean House Guyana are scheduled to open during 1986/87.

From the beginning it was obviously important that the right organisational structure should be created, to ensure the proper development of the self-help initiatives that were to evolve as part of Caribbean House.

It was soon realised that no one structure would do. One of the declared intentions was that the organisation should aim to become self-financing. This ruled out being a registered charity. The structure of a cooperative was considered, but would have been impracticable since some aspects militated against the desired form of management structure. Our goal was to establish an organisation that was neither for profit nor for charity, whose objectives would be to generate its own income from its charitable and educational activities. The only structure that would permit development of this kind of self-help organisation, as envisaged by its founders, was a limited liability company. However, this too would have its drawbacks, as it might prove difficult to attract funding from the normal agencies.

In the end it was decided that the work should be carried out jointly by two inter-related organisations: Caribbean House Group, a registered charity, and Westindian Concern

When one refers to 'Caribbean House', therefore, this means the three main organisations: Westindian Concern Limited, Caribbean House Group and their Education Outreach, Centre for Caribbean Studies.

Westindian Concern Limited

Directors of Westindian Concern
Rev. Dr Ashton Gibson, Founder & Director General
Miss Jocelyn Barrow O.B.E., M.A. (Chairperson)
Mrs Jacqueline Benn
Mrs Grace Gibson
Mr Keith Barker

Westindian Concern Limited was founded in 1975 as a self-help community development project. It differs from other companies in that it has shareholdings and yet is a non-profit organisation. It is responsible for the planning and day to day development of all the activities carried out at Caribbean House. In Westindian Concern no dividends are paid to shareholders, but share investment gives the holder the right to exercise control over policy in direct proportion to the amount of shares held. It also allows paid workers to participate in the management as directors.

Carribean House Group (Registered Charity)

Management Committee of Caribbean House Group
Miss Jocelyn Barrow O.B.E., M.A. (Chairperson)
Rev. Dr. Ashton Gibson Ph.D (Humanities), Director General
Rev. Martin Goodridge, M.A.
Mrs Jacqueline Benn, M.A.
Mrs Daphne Stewart
Mr Olsen Samuels
Mr Patrick Kodikara
Mr Owen Eversley
Mrs Alison Van Horne

This is the associated registered charity of Westindian Concern. It accepts funds on behalf of projects run by the latter, but administers these funds for the purpose for which they are given. The Charity also takes responsibility for the day-to-day running of the family-centred child-care service with its Family Casework and Family Support provisions.

Other activities taking in many aspects of Caribbean cultural lifestyle find expression at Caribbean House, including Caribbean art as well as sport and other recreational activities. Caribbean House Cricket and Domino Teams are among the strongest in the country – the Cricket team are the current holders of the Clive Lloyd Trophy.

Centre for Caribbean Studies

The Centre for Caribbean Studies was established jointly by Westindian Concern Limited and Caribbean House Group as a post-experience teaching and research centre in the field of Westindian Sociology, with a view to understanding the nature and size of the problems facing Westindians and their children in Britain. Its broad aim is to contribute to the development of the theory and practice of public policy, and its activities are directed at those who are involved with the formulation and implementation of policies that affect the well-being of this disadvantaged black minority in Britain. The Centre's methodology includes defining problems, developing solutions, implementing action and evaluating impacts. A number of major research investigations have been carried out by the Centre.

Activities at the Centre include:

Short Courses in Westindian Sociology
The Centre for Caribbean Studies has as one of its purposes the provision of courses for people working in national and local government, statutory and voluntary agencies, e.g., teachers, probation officers, magistrates, community workers, social workers, housing officers, etc.

Courses are arranged to bring together people who have to make judgements of vital importance affecting the wellbeing of people of Westindian origin to help them to understand that simple perceptions and solutions to problems faced by

Westindians require a greater depth of knowledge and understanding than they perhaps realize.

Duration
There are two types of course: (a) a part-time course which requires all-day attendance on six successive Fridays and (b) a week-long block course the content of which is similar to that of Course (a).

Course Content
As far back as 1969, the Institute of Race Relations in a massive report said that 'Westindian children were a source of bafflement, embarrassment and despair to schools.' More recently, as a result of further research carried out by government and voluntary agencies, it has been possible to identify more clearly the area of stress, the particular sectors of the immigrant population with the most severe problems, their effects and the implication for the future if they are not resolved. The course will offer participants a chance to think through the above situation and is divided into two main parts.
1. The Part Time Course consists of six weekly all-day seminars on:
(a) The Family
- Social and Historical background of Westindians.
- Westindian family life and its structure
  a) comparing different attitudes to the family
  b) child-rearing practices among Westindians
  c) adolescence
  d) the elderly
- Culture

(b) Society
- Educational issues; Language
- Racism, individual and institutionalised
- The consequences of Racism, children at risk, and stress-related illnesses.

Individual tutors are assigned and will be available to course members for consultation and guidance.

All successfully completed course work is certificated by the Centre for Caribbean Studies.

Course members may expect to gain considerable insight and understanding into their own decision making and judgements, with a view to improving their effectiveness at both interpersonal and corporate level in their work with

Westindians in Britain.

A pioneeering course entitled *Transcultural Practices: Caring in the 1980s* is now being instituted to offer Social Workers and others much-needed training in transcultural approaches.

Other activities at the Centre include:

Negotiated Activities
Specific staff development, consultancy or research work for individual organisations negotiated in relation to the particular requirements of the agency for the delivery of appropriate services to the Westindian community.

Research
A developing programme of applied research in the field of finding appropriate responses to disadvantage among Afro-Caribbean young people.

Dissemination
The Centre has its own publishing company and produces a series of occasional and working papers in addition to its major publications.

Other User Groups
There are two other major independent groups for which Caribbean House provides the infra-structure and the headquarters; these are the Afro-Westindian United Council of Churches (AWUCOC), a federation of black-led churches in the UK, and the Barbados Overseas Community & Friends Association (BOCFA), a social and cultural organisation.

Caribbean House offers:

1. Statutory and private agencies are invited to take advantage of our specialist knowledge and see as a resource our family-centred child-care service. Family counselling includes a measure of education, Family Casework, Family Support and Intermediate Treatment provisions for children with behavioural problems.

2. We supervise, on behalf of local authorities, children from the following categories:

a) Adolescents subject to care and supervision orders.
b) Adolescents subject to Intermediate Treatment orders.
c) Children in danger of child abuse.

3. A network of black foster parents is available to Social Services Departments in need of this resource.

4. An Anglo-Caribbean Social Services Bureau.
Caribbean House has facilities in the Caribbean for the following:

a) Carrying out enquiries and supervision on behalf of social services departments and provision of care facilities in this region.

b) Providing specialised therapeutic and educational holidays for children of Westindian origin where the more culturally attuned environment of the Caribbean would help to reduce the level of hostility in order to make behavioural changes possible. There are CHE facilities available there.

c) Holiday provisions in the Caribbean with rest home facilities for the elderly.

d) Training and re-orientation programmes for the active elderly.

Appendix B

(This is the abridged text of a paper which I wrote in 1981, before our research had been completed. It was written in direct response to the Interim Report, entitled *West Indian children in our schools*, of the Rampton Committee of Inquiry into the education of children from ethnic minority groups. Many of the comments retain their relevance in respect of *Education for All*, the Committee's final report published in 1985 under the chairmanship of Lord Swann, and almost all the recommendations still apply – A.G.)

The School and the Community – a Westindian View

This paper presents a Westindian view of a Westindian child's journey through the various stages of the educational process, starting at home and going right through to university. It also looks at the relationship between the various institutions involved – notably the school itself – and the community, and how they interact with one another. These remarks are prefaced by an attempt to evaluate, from a Westindian perspective, the conclusiveness of the interim findings of the Rampton Committee of Inquiry.

Firstly, it must be said that the findings of the Interim Report are in many ways weak, ambiguous, imprecise and timidly incomplete, and that the Committee has fudged the real issues in its earnest attempt to be all things to all men. In trying to be nice to everyone they have strayed into the realms of the absurd, going to great lengths to 'sanitise' what from a Westindian point of view is undoubtedly the crux of the matter, the major causal factor behind the underachievement of Westindian children: namely, institutional racism and racial discrimination.

For instance, the Report admits that 'discrimination is still widespread in employment'.[23] But we are not told what the basis of this 'discrimination' is, nor is any definition of the word given to help the reader place it within its proper semantic context.* We are left to infer a meaning according to our prejudices or in line with what we want to believe, which may be well wide of the mark. The discrimination referred to in the Report could conceivably be understood as being practised on the basis of educational qualifications or experience. Such intellectual sophistry merely results in distortion of the central issues, which in turn leads to flawed conclusions.

There has been no attempt to make a systematic empirical exploration of institutional racism and racial discrimination, how these operate in the school process and in the domain of employment and social relations when school-leavers eventually become parents. Does the school experience of these parents engender positive learning practices and attitudes to school socialisation in their children (especially at the early developmental stage in the crucial first five years)? Or does it transmit the opposite? And if so, what are the implications of these factors for teachers and parents?

One of the greatest shortcomings of these interim findings is that little more than a superficial explanation is given concerning the methodology employed in drawing up the report. There is virtually no discussion of the problems and limitations of such an inquiry, no indication as to how the Committee was able to interpret and evaluate the information collected, and therefore no evidence of its reliability or validity. There is some sparse statistical data (purporting to give across-group comparisons of educational performance among school-leavers) to which considerable attention has been paid by the media, and which has apparently been invested with scientific credibility in some quarters. The implications, however, are very serious indeed for the Westindian community, as such data will inevitably be associated with innate intelligence.

The question of differences in educational performance or behaviour between Whites and Blacks (or, more particularly, Westindians) is so deeply politicised that one can hardly read or talk about it without entering the realm, implicit or otherwise, of racism – that is, of white-supremacist ideologies 'scientifically' grounded in genetics and climatology. In view of the current political climate in this country and the existence of

---

* The later Swann Report included definitions of all key words in response to a chorus of criticism on this point.

strong and vociferous extreme right-wing groups, especially the Nazi or neo-Nazi fascist organisations, the need for meticulous care and reponsibility in the field of research has never been greater. It is all too easy, if we fail to exercise this kind of judiciousness, for such people to seize on the results of our research as tools to use for their own ends by selective quoting out of context.

Unhappily, most of the research carried out in this country – whether by academics, politicians or social scientists – either accepts without question the stereotypes to which Westindians have been fitted according to the prevailing prejudice, or else invests such stereotypes with a spurious importance. But anyone prepared to probe sufficiently deep beneath the surface will find the simple and apparently plausible image given to the Westindian starkly at variance with the reality.

For these reasons, among others, the School Leavers Survey from which the offending statistics were drawn should have been presented in its entirety, with an explanation (and full details) of how the sample was taken, what methodology was employed, the theoretical perspective from which it was designed and how the interpretations were arrived at. This, and only this, would have enabled a correct evaluation of the statistics to be made. Also, some sort of caveat should have been printed to the effect that the Survey was in no way a measure of intelligence, innate ability, acquired ability or excellence, in the sample concerned, nor was it a measure of intelligence in racial groups as represented in the sample. Without all these features such a survey can be a dangerous influence and deserves as little credence as a political opinion poll.

Intelligence tests have, like Social Darwinism, become identified with political and social reaction in this country and the USA. Some well-known academics, under the pretext of carrying out scientific research in human developmental psychology and biology, have shamelessly promoted theories which, however euphemistically expressed, seek to validate the political ideology of a 'master race'. The school performance of White and Black children in American schools has tended to be seen in this light, and explanations for differences in achievement have been made in this context. Much the same approach is evident among British academics.

It should scarcely need restating that master-race theories

have given rise to monstrous injustices and persecution of minorities in Europe and the USA. In the late 1920s and early 1930s Lorenz and other European ethnologists, to their everlasting shame, allied themselves in the name of research with the most pernicious ideology in human history: that of Hitler and the Nazis. On the other side of the Atlantic, Termen and Yerkes and their fellow American psychometricians – aided and abetted by eugenicists in biology and racists in politics – succeeded in reducing to a trickle the flow of Jewish immigration that might have saved hundreds of thousands from the gas chambers. This was a classic example of indefensible propaganda being served up as academic research, and it was this spurious respectability which enabled it to influence attitudes so effectively.

From a Westindian (and perhaps also a Black) perspective, therefore, the interim findings of the Committee of Inquiry represent a pernicious, pretentious, pseudo-scholarly attempt to reinforce and justify – albeit unwittingly – stereotype intelligence measurement instruments which are neither objective nor scientific, and whose validity is, therefore, highly questionable.

The human environment is unavoidably social. From the time of their birth human infants are dependent on their mothers and others for biological survival. Psychologically their cognitive, social and emotional development is grounded in human interaction. Adult independence and self-sufficiency are achieved gradually through years of contact and interaction with others. Thus, despite children's sometimes strenuous attempts to resist the pressures of society and family influence, the process of acculturation continues generation after generation. This process, commonly called 'socialisation' by behavioural scientists, is really a form of adaptation and accommodation, since for those who become acceptably socialised there are considerable physical, economic and psychological rewards and benefits to be had; failing to do so means facing ostracism, imprisonment or institutionalisation, or even death. Clearly, therefore, the process of socialisation that begins with birth itself affords continual opportunities for a child's learning to be facilitated, both at home and at school.

The implications of this for teachers, administrators, researchers and politicians, are that family life and other cultural patterns among Westindians must be understood if their young are to reap the benefits of education. Without this understanding very little can be done to educate Westindian children; but such a failure would be a shameful reflection on the teaching profession in this country and its ability to adapt, innovate, and reach out to the young Westindian mind. How many times do we hear teachers (or parents) bemoaning the fact that such-and-such a child 'does not learn', or grumbling, sometimes in genuine desperation, that Westindian children will not or do not want to learn? There is surely no normal, healthy child who does not want to learn, Black or White. Children always want to learn. The remarks of these teachers are therefore an admission of failure on their part: failure to find effective methods of stimulating the minds of their pupils.

All the evidence indicates an overwhelming need to devise new teaching strategies that will bring about such stimulation in Westindian children. There must first be a full appreciation of the ways in which Westindian culture is transmitted through the mother-child interaction. Teacher training should be built around genuinely multi-cultural studies focusing on early infancy, in order to develop theoretical perspectives and empirical research both across and within the various cultures. Study of early childhood development to reveal the origins of cultural programming would provide valuable insights into how children acquire certain patterns of social behaviour, and how they become well-adjusted or maladjusted in terms of their particular culture. This is essential from a moral as well as an educational point of view, since to ignore these factors is to cold-shoulder the Westindian child and to alienate the entire Westindian community.

What, then, is the reality of the situation facing the Westindian child in Britain? Some of the major points, both directly and indirectly concerned with education, are discussed under separate headings below.

Home Background

Because it exercises a great influence on early childhood development, the home offers the best opportunities for the introduction of innovative learning facilities and strategies. However, housing provision for Westindians is at present sub-standard, and must obviously be improved in order that the home environment may be more conducive to learning. One way of achieving this is to ensure better council-housing allocation for Westindians than at present exists, by allowing them an access equal to that of the rest of the population. The same should apply in the job market (both public and private sectors), where genuinely equal opportunities would enable some Westindians to secure better-paid employment and therefore to buy their own houses or rent property that is in a good state of repair and free from damp. This presupposes the eradication of institutional racism and racial discrimination in housing through energetic implementation of the Race Relations Acts, including severer penalties for infringement than those currently being imposed.

Westindian mothers should be given advice, in lectures or through outreach teachers/field-officers, as to what kind of toys to buy for their children – toys with educational value, toys that reflect their heritage, etc. – and what type of games to encourage in order to help them develop learning skills which facilitate the acquisition of knowledge. It is at this early age that educationalists can and should instil in children the skills and habits that will be so useful to them in primary and secondary schools.

Socio-economic and Environmental Factors

The majority of Westindian schoolchildren in Britain come from non-professional families, and more than 90% of the parents are employed in the lowest-paid unskilled jobs. The income of Westindian parents is generally less than that of unskilled White worker-parents, who tend to occupy the higher-paid jobs in that category. Westindians also tend to live in ghetto regions with bad housing, but nevertheless pay higher rents than do the few White people who live in similar areas (which in their case would be called 'slums'). The local schools normally have far less amenities than schools in better-off areas, which tend to be predominantly White, and suffer from a high turnover of teachers, greatly hindering continuity and stability.

Preparation for School

At pre-school level, facilities should be made available for Westindian mothers to send their infants for educational activities and play which will help to prepare them for primary school. These activities should be organised and run by trained nursery-school teachers with the assistance of trained play supervisors, and the team should include some Westindians. This would eliminate much of the trauma suffered by Westindian children on entering primary school.

The proposed programme calls for increased resources in the pre-school field but, since it would almost certainly cause a sharp cut-back in delinquency, such extra outlay would be more than offset by corresponding reductions in the expenditure on social services, residential care, remand school care and, ultimately, prisons. Helping Westindian children to do well at school is to enhance their self-esteem and self-motivation, which will, in turn, make them less likely to turn to crime; instead, their minds will be focused on obtaining the examination results that enable them to go on to the further education of their choice. Today, however, more than two-thirds of all the young people in borstals are Westindian/Black, and in prisons the proportion, though a lot smaller, has risen alarmingly in recent years.

In areas where Westindians live there are pitifully few nursery schools, whilst in better-off districts with a predominantly White population, these are provided in abundance, either by the local authority or by middle-class community groups which charge a fee. Working Westindian mothers (the vast majority) are therefore compelled to rely on commercial child-care services, which are expensive and of no educational value. At such nursery schools as may be accessible, places are over-subscribed and there is almost always a long waiting-list; Westindians continually find themselves at the bottom of this, irrespective of the time they have been on it, while White parents seem to find ways of getting their children placed at comparatively short notice. In many cases allocation methods are a mystery, and it has been known for Westindian children to be offered places after their fifth birthday – which is no use to them as all children are required by law to go to primary school at that age. These are just some of the ways in which valuable potential learning opportunities are denied to the Westindian child who, thus, has far more difficulty than others in settling in when formal education commences.

Primary School

We have become used to considering what is taught and practised in schools as axiomatic and forever immutable. It has also long been accepted as fact that primary school teachers are the people best qualified to teach our children how to read. Fortified by this view, many people in education believe that parents should not start teaching their children before they go to school, as this may create difficulties for teachers. Such insupportable notions have developed out of habitual modes of thinking and out of an understandable desire to protect the professional interest of teachers. It should, however, be perfectly possible for what is taught in schools, as well as how and where it is taught, to be adapted to meet changing circumstances and needs without impairing the learning process.

Multi-Cultural Perspective

Whether intentionally or unintentionally, British schools are giving Westindian pupils complex training in approved images of dominance and deference. When these children leave school at 16 they are not equipped for any job other than those which demand deference or subservience and, if they succeed in getting a job at all, this handicap deprives them of any opportunity to move on.

The traditional curriculum must be changed from its present mono-cultural, ethnocentric – i.e., White-orientated – character, and take on instead a multi-cultural perspective reflecting the reality of society in Britain today. This implies the honest and balanced teaching of Black as well as White history, from the time of the earliest known Black presence in Britain (the Roman occupation) through to the slave trade and, ultimately, the 1950s' wave of immigration. Keeping this as an entirely unemotive issue would enable the emphasis to be placed on the contribution Westindians have made to the economic development of this country: how the slave trade created many of the conditions as well as the capital necessary for the Industrial Revolution to take place, how Westindians played an important part in the post-war reconstruction of Britain, and so on. Given such a historical perspective White children, too, would appreciate the fundamental contribution of Westindians to this country, and this would make it much more difficult for racist agitators to recruit a following in schools and among youth generally.

Changes in the curriculum are, therefore, required at both primary and secondary school level, to make it more pertinent to the background of Westindian and other ethnic minority children, in respect not only of history but of language and culture.

Language

Language is a subject about which Westindians are very defensive. This is because they associate it with class – i.e., those who speak Standard English are seen as belonging to the educated classes. As a result, anyone who speaks a dialect of English will be unlikely to admit that he or she is not speaking English. Also, English Creole speakers largely share a common vocabulary with speakers of Standard English, and this leaves many Westindians, as well as their interlocuters, with the erroneous impression that they already know Standard English. Contrary to widespread belief, especially among officialdom, English is, in effect, the second language of Westindians, Creole or Westindian mesolect (Creole/English) being their first language.

It is, therefore, quite unrealistic of teachers to expect a Westindian child, even one born here, to understand them in the same way as their other pupils do. Small wonder that, when we analyse underachievement among Westindian schoolchildren, language emerges as a significant contributory factor. But, despite all the evidence the authorities, teachers and educational planners have rigidly refused to face up to this fact – although the very same people are quick to acknowledge that English is not the first language of Asian children and readily provide funding for the appropriate extra tuition in their case. For Westindian children too, especially those of primary school age, a programme for the teaching of English as a second language should be instituted, and this should be linked to the teaching of reading and writing in English.

Teachers' Attitudes

The attitude of staff in multi-racial schools is crucial, especially as regards their expectations of children from ethnic minority groups and of Westindians in particular, for the success or failure of a pupil may well depend on it. There must be a greater awareness of Westindian sociology among teachers and educationalists, and this should be incorporated in teacher-training courses as an integral part of multi-cultural studies. However, whatever is to be taught must be devised in close consultation with the Westindian community, and not left to the whims of those who know little or nothing of Westindian culture and history or those who would distort it.

The attitude of teachers cannot be separated from the disproportionate number of Westindian children in special schools, which is testimony to the failure of the British school system. What other explanation could there be for the many factually undeniable phenomena such as London's offsite units for children with behavioural or learning problems being filled almost entirely with Westindian children, while units for truants consist solely of White children? Few teachers realise that truancy among Black children is relatively rare because their parents value education very highly and ensure good attendance. Even where the school fails them and the children are dumped in these special units, they still attend. Perhaps their very attending is ultimately a more effective form of protest than truanting.

An examination of institutional racism within schools is more likely to yield the right answers than tinkering – either with the curricula or with the various forms of teacher-training – that leaves the present education structures intact. This is not to suggest that the system should be radically overhauled, but at least all pay settlements should be suspended until it becomes clear what is required of teachers and whether they are willing to deliver it. This must be doubtful given the fact that so many schools are run or governed by professionals who insist on clinging to their own narrowly traditional and fundamentally racist view of education, quite oblivious to the needs of pupils in a multi-cultural society.

Westindian teachers

Another urgent priority is a teacher-training programme designed to bring about a significant increase in the number of

Westindian teachers. At the moment there are very few teachers of Westindian origin in British schools. While it is somewhat heartening to see some White teachers being sent to the Caribbean to learn about the Westindian way of life, it is correspondingly dismaying that this should be happening when there are so many experienced, but unemployed, Westindian teachers in Britain – a case of an available resource not being tapped.

Examinations and School Assessment

Examinations, like curricula, must be revised and restructured to reflect the multi-cultural nature of society in Britain today, especially in the areas of history, social studies, religious studies and economics.

However, it is in the area of school assessment, be it formal or informal tests or merely the teacher's judgement, that the most radical reforms are needed. Westindians represent an unacceptably high proportion of the intake of schools for ESN and maladjusted children. All too often parents are not informed early enough that their children are in difficulties with their school work, nor are they told in clear terms why this is the case. There is a lot of vagueness in the reasons offered, but generally no explanation of the labels thus attached, nor any outline of the possible remedies. The failure of educators to communicate what they are teaching to Westindian children is clearly neither sufficient reason in itself, nor anything like an objective basis for deciding that these children are ESN or maladjusted. Moreover, the tests used in the assessment procedure, which places so many Westindian children in these categories and thereby effectively consigns them to educational oblivion, have no scientific validity whatsoever.

Pastoral Care and Counselling

There must be an upgrading of individual counselling given to Westindian schoolchildren regarding their personal or school-work problems or their academic career path. This should be done by setting up a monitoring system for each child, allowing for early intervention and enabling problems and difficulties to be detected before the situation deteriorates. However, the idea of pastoral care extending into a child's home through teachers' visits is not viable, as it would almost certainly pose more problems than it could possibly help solve.

In the field of child guidance there are currently very few specialist counselling posts occupied by Westindians. If we are to overcome the many problems besetting Westindian schoolchildren, it is vital for people from the Westindian community itself to be trained for, and become involved in, counselling. Without this it is very unlikely that the educational needs of Westindian children will be met.

Parental Involvement

Many Westindian parents are mistrustful of the role schools play in the education of their children. They see schools as agents of discrimination in the quality of knowledge imparted to Westindian children as compared with pupils from the indigenous population. It is obvious that if schools are to serve and satisfy the aspirations and expectations of Westindian parents – which are generally high regarding their children's school performance – these same schools must institute initiatives to overcome the barriers that exist between them and the Westindian community. Westindian parents should be encouraged to visit schools at reasonable hours, and access to teachers should be made a lot easier than it is at present. All possible modes of communication and interaction should be explored and kept open and, in addition to the standard PTA meetings, regular gatherings should be held to discuss education issues and the concerns of parents, especially Westindians.

Supplementary Schools

In areas of heavy Westindian and Asian settlement, resources should be made available for schools, staffed by specially-trained personnel with a preponderance of Black teachers, to which Westindian and Asian children labelled ESN or maladjusted or disruptive could be sent to continue their education. The Westindian community itself should set up supplementary schools on its own initiative to help those children who are deficient in certain areas of their school work.

This, however, should only be a temporary expedient, since all children are entitled to have their educational needs met within the mainstream of education provisions. Supplementary schools are an affirmation of failure on the part of the school system, and the permanent creation of these for

Westindian or Asian children means institutionalising a palpably unjust situation.

Conclusion

This paper has attempted to outline some of the specific ways in which Westindian and other ethnic minority children can be helped to perform well at school. Beyond specifics, the clear implication is that if these children are to be given genuine, rather than make-believe educational opportunities, there must be fundamental changes at the highest level in thinking, policy formulation/implementation and institutional processes of all kinds. There must also be a far greater willingness to commit resources and to create opportunities in education and employment in both public and private sectors – for the cost to society is certain to be less than the price of not doing so.

Gone forever is the notion that the training children receive in school automatically serves them adequately for the rest of their lives; equally obsolete is the idea that education as a process is restricted to the years of infancy, childhood and youth. The curriculum must therefore not only incorporate a truly multi-cultural perspective, but should be orientated towards the acquisition of adaptive skills, with the emphasis on learning *how to learn*. Westindian children need to be equipped with a repertoire of skills giving them the ability to cope with the information flow and helping them to develop study techniques for the acquisition of knowledge. Were this to happen, the community at large would benefit from increased numbers of Westindian children gaining 'O' and 'A' level qualifications and going on to university, polytechnic or professional training. This would give Westindians far greater social mobility and break down the social barriers that currently inhibit them.

However, it remains to be seen whether the White ruling elite and the society it represents is prepared to share economic as well as political power with the Westindian and other ethnic minority communities. In a society which is essentially class-ridden and dominated by the interests of the majority group, the *status quo* is maintained by a host of inbuilt, self-perpetuating mechanisms, of which the assessment of intelligence through traditional IQ tests is just one example.

Those of us who are teachers bear an awesome threefold

responsibility: firstly to ourselves in upholding our professional integrity, secondly to our pupils and their parents, and thirdly to the community – to ensure that we teach learning skills and impart knowledge to the best of our ability. We must put the teaching of pupils in our charge above all other considerations, irrespective of colour, religion or race. We must not allow ourselves to be used as unwitting agents for the allocation of social status, economic power and political power to particular racial groups, to the neglect and detriment of others.

The problems facing teachers and educational planners, therefore, are not merely problems of pedagogy. They are problems of social justice, of constraints on resources, and of preparing children for life in a rapidly changing multi-racial society. It is not, as some have suggested, that there should be 'positive discrimination' in favour of Westindian children; merely, as empirical evidence shows, that the educational system has failed to make provision for them, and that those operating within it are ill-informed and ill-equipped to meet their special educational needs.

However, in view of the current draconian spending cuts in the field of education, we are perhaps entitled to wonder whether the Rampton/Swann Inquiry is just an exercise in keeping up appearances, rather than a genuine and serious effort to help Westindian and other ethnic minority schoolchildren.

Appendix C

October, 1985

The spotlight was being turned on Westindians in a big way at the time this book went to press, mainly on account of the rioting in London and Birmingham. There were troubles surrounding two principals of educational establishments who had publicly made racist remarks: Ray Honeyford (Drummond Middle School, Bradford), about ethnic minority pupils in general, and Jack Fuller (Waltham Forest College) about Westindian youths. And a major report from Keele University, entitled *The Educational and Vocational Experiences of 15- to 18-year-old young people of ethnic minority groups* (the Eggleston Report – a great improvement on the Swann Report), echoed most of the findings of our own investigation.

The net effect has been that many more people have begun to sit up and take notice where previously their heads have been firmly planted in the sand. This is partly because the media have taken up the cudgels with a vengeance, something they tend to do the moment an issue becomes 'newsworthy' (though they often rapidly lose interest and rejoin the ostriches). In this context it is well worth quoting the *Guardian* leader of 17 October:

Nicely timed to coincide with the Honeyford row in Bradford and the growing troubles at the Waltham Forest college in north-east London comes the heavyweight Eggleston report, The Educational and Vocational Experiences of Young Black Britons. To summarise a major study in a few sentences is asking for trouble. But in brief: Black and Asian pupils show a quite impressive determination to press on towards higher education, in spite of formidable obstacles. High among those obstacles is the fact that teachers tend to place pupils from the ethnic minorities on courses 'significantly below those appropriate for their abilities and ambitions.' In particular, teachers expect less from Black students than they would from Whites or Asians. The net result is a 'self-fulfilling prophecy'. Blacks live down to expectations whilst other groups forge ahead.

Again and again the Eggleston team come back to the thought that teachers should pay attention to the context in which they formulate and express judgements. 'Our evidence suggests that some teachers need reminding of the implications and consequences of their behaviour in their work with children from a range of ethnic backgrounds.' Mr Ray Honeyford, headmaster of the Drummond Middle School in Bradford, and Mr Jack Fuller, principal of the Waltham Forest College, could do worse than write out 500 times apiece that simple sentence. Both men deserve censure above all for the slap happy manner and the context in which they went about expressing simplistic but by no means wicked or illegitimate opinions.

Mr Honeyford says that, if a school contains a disproportionate (his word) number of children for whom English is a second language or from homes where educational ambition and the values to support it are conspicuously absent, then academic standards are bound to suffer. He makes it painfully clear that, for him, 'Asians' fit the first category and 'West Indians' the second. Mr Fuller complains about 'snatches' and petty theft on campus. The culprits are, he suggests, West Indian youths from off campus. But then he adds in a recent letter to *The Times*, that he had witnessed the 'loud aggressive conduct seen in Britain' in the course of a recent trip to Jamaica.

There is a deal of stereotyping about the Honeyford thesis, and, as Eggleston demonstrates, pretty suspect stereotyping at that. Asians do not merely want to achieve. They do achieve and, in doing so, they often raise academic averages. Black students and their parents have ambitions which are not being fulfilled – in good part because of the automatic, damning assumptions made by some teachers. To label a child culturally inferior is as damaging as to label him or her genetically inferior. Equally, to identify a problem of petty theft, to note (if it is indeed the case) that Black kids are disproportionately involved – but then to bang on about the impressionistic, 'what I did on my holidays' Jamaican nature of this loutishness is merely subversive of confidence within a multi racial college only a matter of miles and days from Tottenham.

Eggleston suggests there comes a point at which teachers have to consider 'whether or not they are still suitable to be members of the profession.' Messrs Honeyford and Fuller are most assuredly not at that point. But they are, of their volition, at the point where they should consider whether continued service at their current, heavily 'ethnic' institutions is in the interests of those they are appointed to serve – the children and students, White and Black alike.

One can only hope that the message (both the overt and the implicit) has not fallen on deaf ears.

Notes

1. *Education for All*, HMSO, 1985, pp. 86–87.
2. E. J. B. Rose *et al.*, *Colour and Citizenship*, OUP, 1969, p. 281.
3. *Ibid*, pp. 283–5.
4. *Ibid*, pp. 285–6.
5. *The Observer*, c. 1972 (material quoted from author's original manuscript).
6. *Ibid.*
7. *Ibid.*
8. *West Indian children in our schools*, HMSO, 1981, p. 12.
9. *Ibid*, p. 10.
10. *Ibid*, p. 11.
11. *Education for All*, p. 81.
12. *Ibid*, p. 29.
13. *Ibid*, p. 30.
14. *Ibid*, p. 84.
15. *Ibid*, p. 329.
16. *Ibid*, p. 769.
17. *Education for All*, p. 28.
18. *Westindian children in our schools*, p. 14.
19. G. W. Allport, 'Attitudes' in *Handbook of Social Psychology*, ed. Murchison (Clark University Press, Worcester, Mass. and OUP, London, 1935).
20. D. D. Droba, 'The Nature of Attitude', *J. Social Psychology*, Vol. IV, 1933, pp. 444–63.
21. C. W. Blackmann and P. F. Secord, *Problems in Social Psychology* (McGraw-Hill, New York, 1966).
22. C. W. and M. Sherif, *Attitude, Ego, Involvement and Change* (Pennsylvania Univ. Press, Westport, Connecticut).
23. *Westindian children in our schools*, p. 52.

Centre for Caribbean Studies Publications

A LIGHT IN THE DARK TUNNEL (Westindian Concern/Caribbean House 10th Anniversary Volume)
by Ashton Gibson and Charles Lewis

A CLASH OF CULTURES (An Examination of the differences between Westindian and English Family Life)
by Ashton Gibson

THE EYE OF THE STORM (The Education of Westindians in British Schools)
by Ashton Gibson

LANGUAGE IDENTITY AND THE WESTINDIAN CHILD
by Dennis Craig

PREGNANCY AMONG UNMARRIED WESTINDIAN TEENAGERS
by Ashton Gibson

THE RELATIONSHIP BETWEEN THE POLICE AND THE WESTINDIAN COMMUNITY
by Ashton Gibson

SOCIAL SERVICES: A BANE TO THE WESTINDIAN COMMUNITY
by Ashton Gibson

A HANDBOOK OF THE AFRO-WESTINDIAN UNITED COUNCIL OF CHURCHES
A Resource for Professional People wishing to make contact with the grass roots of the Westindian population through self-help oriented Black-led Churches.

READERS NOTES

READERS NOTES

READERS NOTES

READERS NOTES

READERS NOTES

READERS NOTES

READERS NOTES

READERS NOTES

READERS NOTES

READERS NOTES